Energy resources and economic development in India

Energy resources and economic development in India

WALLACE EDWARD TYNER
Purdue University

Martinus Nijhoff Social Sciences Division
Leiden | Boston 1978

Distributors for North America
Kluwer Boston Inc.
160 Old Derby Street
Hingham, MA 02043 USA

ISBN 90.207.0755.8

Printed in the Netherlands.

Preface

The purpose of this research has been to explore the relationship between energy resource development and economic development in India. The thesis which evolved from the research is that energy resource development has lagged behind and constrained economic development in India. Inadequate attention has been paid to developing the power sector, and the petroleum sector is just beginning to be developed. This research consists of an analysis of energy supply covering each of the major energy resources.

Using information from India's five year plans, the history of energy resource development was compiled by energy sector. A comprehensive evaluation of India's current position with respect to energy resources was undertaken to provide a perspective on future development possibilities. Alternative policy options were presented in the analysis of each energy resource. These options were considered in providing a set of overall policy suggestions for development of energy supplies in India.

Dedication

This volume is dedicated to my wonderful wife, Jean, who patiently endured the weeks, months and years it took to complete. No words can express my feelings for her and the sacrifices she has made, but this token gesture is the least I can do.

Acknowledgements

This research was done under the supervision of Professor John Adams. Throughout the research and writing he provided able guidance and very helpful suggestions and comments. The author is very grateful for having had the opportunity to work with him in this undertaking. His quick mind and perceptive insights have been an invaluable contribution to the research effort.

The author is grateful to the Center for International Studies, Cornell University for providing a research and travel grant to finance a portion of this research. Professor Robert Kalter of Cornell University provided helpful advice in developing the computer model, and John Broderick provided programming assistance. Professor John Mellor of Cornell assisted in arrangements for the trip to India and stimulated my thinking on several topics. Numerous officials of the Government of India gave generously of their time and had a significant impact on my thinking on many of the issues raised in the study. Ann D'Abbracci patiently typed the entire manuscript several times, and Jean Tyner provided valuable assistance in proof reading the paper. The author is indebted to all of these individuals for their assistance. Of course, any errors that remain are entirely the responsibility of the author.

Table of contents

PREFACE V

DEDICATION. VII

ACKNOWLEDGEMENTS. VIII

LIST OF TABLES XIII

LIST OF FIGURES XV

I. INTRODUCTION 1

Energy Consumption and National Income 1
Energy Consumption and National Income in the Development Context 3
India – the focus of analysis 3
Energy consumption and national income in India 3
Energy Supply and Economic Growth 5
The link between energy availability and economic growth . . . 5
Energy supply and unbalanced growth 6
Organization and Contents 9
India's energy resource endowment 9
Energy resource development in the five year plans 9
Oil and natural gas 10
Power. 10
Biogas and solar energy sources 11
Conclusions and policy recommendations 11

II. ENERGY RESOURCE ENDOWMENTS OF INDIA 12

Energy Consumption 12
Alternative measures of aggregate energy consumption 12
Energy consumption patterns 15
Coal 19
Oil and Natural Gas 22
Hydropower 24
Nuclear Energy Resources 27
Non-Commercial Energy Sources 28
Other Energy Sources 29
Solar energy 29
Alternative energy sources 30
Summary 30

III. ENERGY RESOURCE DEVELOPMENT IN THE FIVE YEAR PLANS . . . 32

Electric Power 32
First Five Year Plan (1951-1956) 32
Second Five Year Plan (1956-1961) 33
Third Five Year Plan (1961-1966) 33
Fourth Five Year Plan (1969-1974) 34
Summary of first four plans 35
Fifth Five Year Plan (1974-1979) 37
Coal 38
First Five Year Plan 38
Second Five Year Plan 39
Third Five Year Plan 40
Fourth Five Year Plan 40
Summary of first four plans 41
Fifth Five Year Plan 42
Oil and Natural Gas 42
Nuclear Energy 43
Summary 44

IV. OIL AND NATURAL GAS 45

Brief History of the Oil Industry in India 45
Current Structure of Oil Operations in India 46
Production Sharing Contracts 47

General provisions 47
Tax provisions 50
Resource Leasing Policy Evaluation Model 51
The exploration phase of resource development 55
Uncertainty and the Monte Carlo analysis. 55
Future resource prices 58
Investment cost contingency factor 59
Operating cost contingency factor. 59
Presence or absence of resources 60
Amount of reserves 60
Model description with Monte Carlo simulation. 61
Economic, engineering, and geologic relationships 62
Monte Carlo results and model outputs 72
Model summary 73
Analytical Results 74
Assumptions and data inputs 76
Simulation results. 78
Summary 85
Policy Recommendations 87

V. ELECTRIC POWER 89

Recent Power Shortages 89
Forecasting Power Demand and Generating Capacity Requirements. 92
Terms used in describing electric power. 92
Forecasting relationships 93
Forecasting procedures used in India 95
Bias in the forecasting procedures 96
Forecast modifications 99
Power Development in India 100
Hydropower 101
Coal 104
Organization of the coal industry 104
Coal consumption in India 106
Nuclear power 107
Rural Electrification. 108
Summary 109

VI. BIOGAS AND OTHER ALTERNATIVE ENERGY SOURCES 111

Biogas Based Power Generation 111
Cost of centralized power generation 113
Biogas based power generation 115
Comparison of cost estimates 119
Biogas Fuel Generation. 120
Potential Problems with a Biogas Generation Program 122
Solar Energy 124

VII. CONCLUSIONS AND POLICY RECOMMENDATIONS 125

Oil and Natural Gas. 125
Power Development 126
Hydropower 127
Coal 128
Nuclear 128
Alternative rate structures 129
Alternative Energy Sources 129
Biogas 129
Solar energy. 130
Non-commercial Energy 131
Energy and the Environment 132
Energy Policy Recommendations 133

SELECTED BIBLIOGRAPHY 136

List of tables

1. National Income and Energy Consumption Data for India, 1953-54 to 1970-71 4
2. Coal Equivalent and Coal Replacement Values for Selected Energy Sources 14
3. Energy Consumption Shares for 1970-71 of Major Fuels Using Three Different Measures 14
4. Consumption of Commercial Energy Resources in 1973 for Selected Countries 15
5. Energy Consumption in India in 1970-71 by Sector and Energy Source 16
6. Energy Consumption in the United States in 1971 by Sector and Energy Source 17
7. Average Properties of Coal Fuels 20
8. Coal Reserves of India 21
9. Coal Reserves and Production of Selected Countries and Regions 23
10. Oil Reserves and Production of Selected Countries and Regions . 25
11. Regional Distribution of Hydropower Potential and Development 26
12. Hydropower Capacity by Type of Project 26
13. Hydropower Resources of Selected Countries 27
14. Third Plan Expenditures for Electric Power Generation and Distribution 34
15. Outlay for Power During the Fourth Plan 35
16. Expenditure on Power Development During the Plans 36
17. Growth of Installed Capacity by Type of Plan 37
18. Planned and Actual Increases in Installed Generating Capacity 1951-1974 37
19. Planned Generating Capacity Additions During the Fifth Plan . 38
20. Planned Expenditures for Power During the Fifth Plan 38
21. Coal Production in India 41
22. Share Structure for Profit Oil 48

23. Input Variables for the Generalized Resource Policy Model . . 54
24. Distributions Used for Uncertain Variables. 57
25. Common Input Values for Leasing Policy Analysis 76
26. Results of Model Simulations 80
27. Model Simulations in the Indian Setting 84
28. Standard Deviation-Mean Ratios for Alternative Systems . . . 84
29. Regions and States Seriously Affected by Power Shortages 1974-75 90
30. Percentage Changes in Production in Selected Industries for the Period January-August, 1972 to 1974 91
31. Per Capita Power Consumption and Power Losses by State . . 94
32. Forecasts of Power Consumption and Requirement and Required Installed Capacity for the Firth Plan 98
33. Estimates of Coal Requirement for 1978-79. 106
34. Progress in Rural Electrification in India 109
35. Unit Cost of Centralized Electricity Supply in India 115
36. Assumptions Used for Biogas Power Generation 117
37. Costs of a Decentralized Biogas Generation and Electrification Plant 118
38. Fuel Energy Available from Private Biogas Units. 121
39. Alternative Policies for Developing India's Offshore Oil Resources 135

List of figures

1. Effect of SOC Investment on DPA Investment 8
2. Flow Diagram for Simulation Model with Endogenous Q_0 . . . 52
3. Flow Diagram for Simulation Model with Input Q_0 53
4. Normal Distribution Used for Annual Price Change and Reserves 57
5. Triangular Distribution. 57
6. Uniform Distribution 57
7. Lognormal Distribution 58
8. Production Profile Through Time 64
9. Solution to the Economic Time Horizon 67

1. Introduction

What Lord Macaulay said about science in his essay on Sir Francis Bacon also could be said of energy:

> . . . it has lighted up the night with the splendor of the day, it has extended the range of the human vision, it has multiplied the power of the human muscles, it has accelerated motion, it has annihilated distance, it has facilitated intercourse, correspondence, all friendly offices and all despatch of business, it has enabled man to descend to the depths of the sea, to soar into the air, to penetrate securely into the noxious recesses of the earth, to traverse the land in cars which whirl along without horses, and the ocean in ships which run ten knots an hour against the wind.[1]

Clearly, increasing energy consumption has been linked with economic progress. This study examines this relationship more closely in the context of economic development, and evaluates energy resource development strategies for various energy producing sectors.

ENERGY CONSUMPTION AND NATIONAL INCOME

To begin this study, we will explore in some detail the relationship between energy consumption and national income. Using 1961 data on all 153 then existing world countries, Fremont Felix showed that national income per capita and total commercial energy consumption per capita are closely related.[2] More recently Darmstadter *et al.* looked at the correlation between energy consumption and national income using both time series and cross-sectional data. They stated their basic conclusion as follows:

> A prominent characteristic of per capita consumption of commercial energy forms is its systematic and quantitatively close association with indicators of general economic development, measured here by per capita GNP – that is, an area's production of all goods and services per person. This relationship between GNP and energy holds both cross-sectionally and historically:

1. Walter H. French and Gerald D. Sanders, eds., *The Reader's Macaulay* (New York: American Book Company, 1936), p. 312.
2. Felix Fremont, 'Growth of Energy Consumption and National Income Throughout the World,' *IEEE Spectrum* (July 1964): 81-102.

the higher a nation's income or output on the current international scale, the higher, in general, its level of energy consumption; as its GNP rises over time, so does its energy consumption – in close, even if not proportionate, conformity.[3]

The authors recognized that, 'Although the connection between energy consumption and GNP may be more or less self-evident, the chain of causation between these two factors is less distinct...'[4] Energy inputs such as electric power and coal are required to support a growing industrial sector. The ready availability of cheap energy may serve to stimulate industrial development. Energy has been called the fuel of economic progress. Conversely, progress in energy intensive industrial development will lead to increased energy production and consumption per capita. Increasing living standards lead to increasing energy consumption because of comfort needs that must be satisfied by energy intensive devices such as automobiles, appliances, and air conditioning. Although the direction of causation cannot be established by the existence of a statistical relationship between income and energy consumptio-n, it is useful to examine the degree of correlation.

Using income per capita (Y/P) and commercial energy consumption per capita (E/P) for 1965 for forty-nine countries having per capita income of at least \$300, Darmstadter produced the regression relationship given in equation 1:

(1) $\text{Log } E/P = -0.34 + 1.12 \text{ Log } Y/P$

The correlation coefficient was .87 ($R^2 = .76$), the F ratio was 141, and the significance level was 0.1 percent. Equation 2 gives the cross-section regression results for twenty-four countries with per capita income levels ranging between \$300 and \$899.

(2) $\text{Log } E/P = -1.93 + 1.79 \text{ Log } Y/P$

The correlation coefficient was .70 ($R^2 = .49$), the F ratio was 21, and the level of significance was 0.1 percent. Darmstadter achieved similar results using average growth rates for the period 1925-1965 for twelve advanced countries.[5]

3. Joel Darmstadter with Perry D. Teitelbaum and Jaroslav G. Polach, *Energy in the World Economy: A Statistical Review of Trends in Output, Trade, and Consumption Since 1925* (Baltimore: Johns Hopkins Press-R.F.F., 1971), p. 32.
4. Ibid.
5. Ibid., p. 868.

ENERGY CONSUMPTION AND NATIONAL INCOME IN THE DEVELOPMENT CONTEXT

All of the countries included in the Darmstadter analysis had per capita incomes greater than $300. This study is concerned with the relationship between energy supply and economic development of a country with per capita income much below this level. Surprisingly little research has been devoted to the relationships between energy resource development and economic growth in less developed countries. A plausible explanation for this situation has been provided by Vadilal Dagli:

> Too often, the question of exploitation of our natural resources tends to fall between two stools. The economists have paid inadequate attention to this important subject because they generally lack the necessary knowledge of the technology of production without which it is not possible to discuss these problems properly. On the other hand, the technologists lack the macro-economic view which is necessary for this purpose. Their very specialisation also prevents them from taking a broader view even at the technological level.[6]

This study will attempt to close this gap by drawing upon the latest and most reliable technical information available in disciplines such as geology and engineering. This information will be used in a framework suitable for economic policy analysis and development planning.

India – the focus of analysis

India was selected as the focus of the analysis for a number of reasons. India has a large industrial base, yet most of her people are engaged in agricultural activities. Although India is not resource poor, she does not possess an abundance of oil and natural gas which would place her in the group of resource rich developing nations. On the other hand, with adequate investment in resource development, India potentially has a resource base sufficient to produce much of the energy needed to fuel her future growth. Consequently, energy supply policy could be crucial to future resource development and economic growth in India. Beyond these reasons, the author has a long standing interest in India, her people, and their struggle for economic progress.

Energy consumption and national income in India

It is interesting to determine if the same close relationship between energy consumption and national income previously described holds in the Indian context. To investigate this hypothesis, total commercial energy consumption

6. Vadilal Dagli, *Natural Resources in the Indian Economy* (Bombay: Vora and Co., 1971), p. 1.

and national income (at 1961-62 prices) for the eighteen year period from 1953-54 to 1970-71 was used. The data for this analysis are contained in Table 1. National income is expressed as a function of energy consumption. Both the log-log and linear forms gave very good fits; the linear form is shown in equation 3:

$$(3) \qquad Y = 68.90 + .592\,E$$

	(2.84)	(.022)	standard errors
	24.3	26.6	T values

Durbin-Watson = 1.97

where E is total energy consumption in million tons of coal replacement (defined in Chapter 2) and Y is national income (at 1960-61 prices) in billions

Table 1. National income and energy consumption data for India, 1953-54 to 1970-71.

Year	National income in 1960-61 prices (billions of Rupees)	Commercial energy consumption (million tons of coal replacement)
1953-54	102.02	60.11
1954-55	104.83	62.67
1955-56	108.60	68.50
1956-57	114.61	72.06
1957-58	112.54	80.33
1958-59	121.65	85.43
1959-60	123.99	91.17
1960-61	132.67	101.16
1961-62	137.32	111.98
1962-63	139.94	126.20
1963-64	147.69	130.02
1964-65	158.84	136.47
1965-66	150.81	146.97
1966-67	152.57	154.58
1967-68	166.16	164.61
1968-69	171.80	176.73
1969-70	181.52	191.74
1970-71	190.35	197.19

Sources: Energy Consumption Data, G.o.I., *Report of the Fuel Policy Committee*, pp. 126-130; National Income Data, G.o.I., *Economic Survey – 1974-75*, p. 59; and *Times of India, Directory and Yearbook Including Who's Who – 1976*, p. 596.

of Rupees.[7] The simple correlation was .99; adjusted R^2, .98; F ratio, 710; and the significance level, 0.1 percent.

Clearly, there was a very close correspondence between national income and energy consumption in India during the time period represented by this data. The work of Darmstadter and Felix indicates that this correspondence is widespread and continues through advanced stages of development.

The close correspondence between income and energy consumption in the Indian data again brings up the question of causation. One might argue that the correspondence only indicates that increasing economic activity stimulates greater energy consumption, and therefore, national planners need not concern themselves with energy supply issues. It is our contention, however, that at least in the Indian context, energy does matter, that inadequate supplies of energy can inhibit development, and that assurance of an adequate supply and mix of energy inputs can be a great stimulus to development.

ENERGY SUPPLY AND ECONOMIC GROWTH

A major theme to be developed here is that availability of ample energy supplies can provide a stimulus to economic development. While changes in energy consumption and national income certainly are interrelated, a strong case can be made for the causative link from adequate energy supplies to economic growth, especially in developing countries such as India.

The link between energy availability and economic growth

The close correspondence between energy consumption and national income in both cross-sectional and time series data implies that inadequate energy supplies could inhibit economic growth. Power shortages in recent years in India have affected a wide range of economic activity in both the industrial and agricultural sectors. Coal shortages have caused curtailments in steel production and electric power generation. Fertilizer production has been

7. The regression using the log-log form is shown below:

$Ln\ Y =$	2.630 +	.486 $Ln\ E$	
	(.087)	(.018)	Standard errors
	30.3	26.5	T values
	Durbin-Watson = 1.90		

The simple correlation was .99; adjusted R^2, .98; F ratio, 703; and the significance level, 0.1 percent.

adversely affected by inadequate energy supplies. Since 1974, the drastic price increases and supply constraints on petroleum products have also caused disruptions in transport and industrial activity. Inadequate energy supplies can result in lower industrial and agricultural production and reduce the rate of economic growth.

In addition, uncertainty regarding future adequacy of energy supplies could be a deterrent to both private and public sector investment in the current period. In other words, a high degree of uncertainly regarding future availability and cost of energy would be a deterrent to investment in activities which are highly dependent on energy inputs. Expectations of energy shortages could certainly a reduction in investment levels. Similarly, expectations of abundant energy supplies at reasonable costs could provide a stimulus to investment. Therefore, both current production levels and investment levels which reflect future production potential are dependent on reliable energy supplies. Energy supply policy should be an important consideration for development planners since adequate supplies of energy are an important component, if not prerequisite, of sustained economic growth.

Energy supply and unbalanced growth

It may be helpful to place this discussion in the unbalanced growth framework developed by A. O. Hirschman using his categories of Social Overhead Capital (SOC) and Directly Productive Activities (DPA). Hirschman includes power supply in the SOC category, and presumably other forms of energy also fall into this category. He argues that imbalances in the provision of one or the other category of investments can lead to 'induced investment' in the other category. For example, provision of an adequate supply of power at reasonable prices could induce power intensive DPA investments. DPA investment is induced because of external economies provided by the (SOC) power generation investments. The expected profitability of power consumptive investments is enhanced if the anticipated energy supply picture is improved. This process is called a 'permissive sequence' because the ready availability of power 'permits' but does not 'compel' sequential DPA investment.

On the other hand, an excess of DPA investments in power intensive industries could also induce SOC investment in power production. Shortages of power would cause production problems and higher costs in the DPA sector, and political pressure on public authorities and agencies would lead to more investment in (SOC) power generation facilities. This sequence is called the 'compulsive' sequence because DPA investments are said to 'compel' further SOC investments.[8]

Hirschman tends to argue that this sequence of development (via SOC shortages) is more powerful because, 'A shortage... is bound to lead to attempts to remedy it on the part of those who suffer from it or who stand to gain from its elimination.'[9] On the other hand, he argues, 'There is no doubt that neglect of public utilities can become a most serious drag on economic progress... that there is a minimum SOC/DPA output ratio, i.e., a point where DPA output can only be increased if SOC is expanded.'[10] One interpretation of the argument being developed here is that India is continually near this limit and that a significant expansion of energy resource development investments (SOC) could induce substantial DPA investments and increase the rate of economic growth.

Inadequate energy supplies, power curtailments, transport bottlenecks, and other SOC constraints can quickly turn an anticipated supra-marginal investment to a sub-marginal investment. In the context of Hirschman's discussion of profit expectations and liquidity preferences, inadequate supply or uncertainty in the future availability of power or other SOC outputs could make a significant difference in the level of today's DPA investment.[11] Figure 1 shows the potential difference in levels of DPA investment with alternative expectations regarding future profitability caused by different levels of SOC investment.

Line A represents profit expectations with uncertainty in future power supply, and the intersection with I-I yields an investment level of I_a. With anticipated adequate supplies of energy and power, line B represents the higher expected profit rate, and the intersection with I-I yields the higher level of DPA investment I_b.

To the extent that the Indian private sector is depended upon for the DPA investment, chances are the DPA investment would not proceed to a superabundant level where a SOC shortage would 'compel' further development. To the contrary, a SOC shortage could simply decrease the level of DPA investment. *In a country accustomed to vicious circles of shortage, there is nothing compelling about a new shortage.* The pressure of added shortages could reinforce feelings of despair and reconfirm the attitude that efforts to break the

8. Albert O. Hirschman, *The Strategy of Economic Development* (New Haven: Yale University Press, 1958), pp. 62-97.
9. Ibid., p. 93.
10. Ibid., p. 96.
11. Ibid., pp. 20-24.

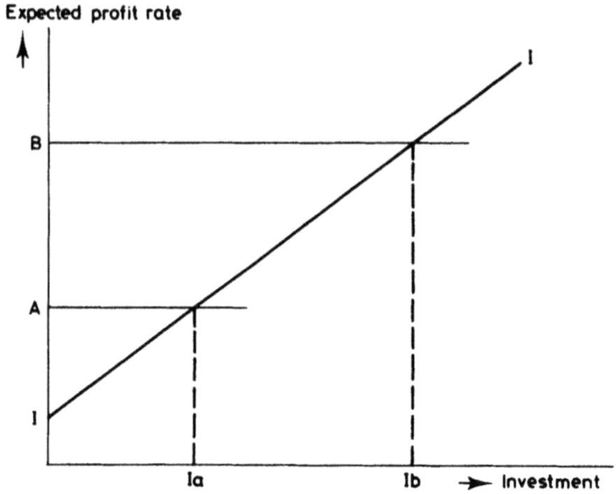

Figure 1. Effect of SOC investment on DPA investment.

vicious cycle will be fruitless. Toward the end of his book, Hirschman reflects on the potential pitfalls in reliance on pressures and shortages:

> Looking back upon the main thesis of this book, I cannot help feeling a little uneasy about the importance and creative virtue that I have bestowed on pressures, tensions, and disequilibrium. Actually the argument is no more than an extension of the familiar view which makes economic growth dependent on a continuing outcropping of profitable opportunities. These are, after all, also disequilibria which induce constructive action. But our extension of the concept of disequilibrium to include situations replete not only with opportunities to be grasped but with hindrances, difficulties, and other types of tension, raises the question whether the response to such situations is not at times going to be destructive and whether the process that has been sketched is not therefore a rather risky affair.[12]

Also, as Hirschman points out, in many cases SOC investments may be safer because they are diversified investments in the general growth of the economy. Capacity additions to an interconnected electric power system are one such example.[13] Increased oil and natural gas production is another. In fact, many, if not most, potential investments in energy supply development fall into this category.

The chapters that follow will reiterate the importance of energy availability in maintaining and increasing the productive capacity of the Indian economy. Using Hirschman's unbalanced growth framework, our purpose here has been to argue that SOC investments in energy supply augmentation can be a

12. Ibid., p. 208.
13. Ibid., p. 85.

powerful force to induce future DPA investments, that energy and power abundance can be an effective stimulus to economic growth.

ORGANIZATION AND CONTENTS

This study is divided into seven chapters and covers each of the major energy resources available to India. The length of each chapter is not proportionate to the importance of the energy sector. The depth of analysis of each sector is determined by data availability and the author's interest. For example, solar energy may be extremely important in the future in India, but little attention is given to it here because of the paucity of data.

Since this study is concerned with energy supply alternatives, each of the major resource chapters stands alone. Other than the general policy framework, analysis of oil and gas resource development has little in common with the analysis of power development or development of other alternatives. Hence, the bulk of this study consists of independent analyses of resource development for each of the major resources. The final chapter summarizes the major conclusions in each energy sector and integrates these conclusions into a policy framework for the energy sector as a whole.

India's energy resource endowment

Following the Introduction, Chapter 2 summarizes the potential magnitude of energy resources in India available for development. The chapter begins by describing and defining the alternative measurement systems used to aggregate data on energy consumption and energy supplies. Data on proven, probable, and speculative reserves of oil, natural gas, coking and non-coking coal, hydropower, and nuclear energy sources are compiled and evaluated. This data is used in subsequent chapters which evaluate current and potential policies regarding energy resource development.

Energy resource development in the five year plans

Chapter 3 provides a general review of energy resource development through the five year plans. Programs and investments in the first three plans are briefly sketched, and a more comprehensive analysis is provided for the energy sector in the fourth and fifth plans. The analysis is organized by energy resource with plans and progress for each major energy resource being followed through the first four plans up to the present time (fifth plan). The background information in this chapter sets the stage for the subsequent analysis of future policy directions by energy resource.

Oil and natural gas

Oil and natural gas resource development policy is crucial to India's future development plans. Currently, petroleum imports absorb about 40 percent of India's foreign exchange earnings. Petroleum products are being taxed at a very high rate; the price of gasoline is about $2.00 per U.S. gallon.[14] The effects on petroleum consuming industries and the transport sector have been devastating. It is clear that public investment which could result in increased domestic supplies of crude oil and natural gas would stimulate production and investment in other sectors of the economy and free vital foreign exchange resources for other uses.

Chapter 4 examines alternatives available to the Indian government for inceasing supplies of petroleum. Following a brief history of the petroleum industry in India, the current structure of oil operations is reviewed. With the recent successes of public sector exploration and development of petroleum resources, expansion of public sector investments in this area is one policy alternative.

Another alternative is leasing potential petroleum bearing areas to foreign private sector companies. To evaluate the viability of this alternative, the Indian leasing system was modeled and compared with leasing systems being used in other countries. A discounted cash flow simulation model was developed and used for this analysis. A complete description of the model and the simulation results are contained in Chapter 4. The chapter concludes with policy recommendations for development of oil and natural gas resources.

Power

Chapter 5 provides an analysis of the electric power sector beginning with a description of the effects of recent power shortages on the Indian economy. Both the industrial and agricultural sectors in several regions have been adversely affected by power outages. There is evidence that production in many industries has been reduced by power shortages; consequently, economic growth has declined.

14. Interviews with Professor S. Chakravarty, Planning Commission and Chairman of the Fuel Policy Committee, and Mr. T. L. Sankar, Secretary of the Fuel Policy Committee, New Delhi, India, December 1975.

Following the discussion of power shortages, the next step was to evaluate the procedures used to forecast power generating requirements for five year plans. The forecasts are calculated by relating future income and production expectations with power consumption and income and production patterns over the recent past. In other words, a type of trend forecast is used. To the extent that shortages have existed in the recent past, this procedure amounts to planning for future shortages. The existing forecasts were modified, and the implications of the revised forecasts determined.

The next section of Chapter 5 covers power development in India from each of the power sources: hydropower, coal based thermal generation, and nuclear power. Problems with hydropower development and the future prospects are evaluated. The past and present organization of the coal industry is described and the potential for increased coal production for power generation evaluated. The last section of this chapter reviews the problems, progress, and prospects for rural electrification in India.

Biogas and solar energy sources

One potential alternative to centralized power generation for rural electrification is local biogas power generation. This process is evaluated and the costs of centralized and decentralized rural electrification are compared. A number of potential social and administrative problems which will arise if a program is developed to establish biogas units for village operation are discussed and evaluated. Biogas units could also be used to produce cooking fuel and fertilizer alone, and this potential is also explored.

In addition to biogas, other nonconventional energy sources could be used in India. One major candidate is solar energy. Both biogas and solar energy have the potential of providing energy supplies to remote areas, and thereby stimulating other productive activities.

Conclusions and policy recommendations

The final chapter provides conclusions and policy recommendations for the energy sector in India. Specific conclusions are summarized for oil and natural gas development and power development. Conclusions with respect to the potential for biogas and solar energy are also presented. The future role of non-commercial energy in India is discussed in the context of the increasing development of commercial energy. The study concludes with a general assessment of the role of energy resource development in the economic development of India.

2. Energy resource endowments of India

This chapter outlines the energy resources of India. Alternative measures for aggregate energy consumption are presented, and current consumption patterns are reviewed. Resource estimates are developed for coal, oil and natural gas, hydropower potential, nuclear fuels, non-commercial energy and other energy sources. A classification scheme appropriate for each resource has been adopted. The resource endowments described in this chapter will be used later in conjunction with planning practices for an analysis of future energy resource development strategies.

ENERGY CONSUMPTION

Alternative measures of aggregate energy consumption

For policy analysis it is sometimes useful to combine energy consumption from different sources into one consumption value. Three measurement systems have been used to aggregate different types of energy consumption. The simplest of these is the *heat content* system. This measure is formed by determining the average heat value of locally available coal (in kilocalories) and converting other energy sources into heat units based on their energy (heat) content. The heat content system does not take into account differences in efficiency of utilization among the various energy sources.

The most commonly used system internationally is the *coal equivalent* system. United Nations data on energy consumption is reported using this measure. The coal equivalent measure uses heat content for energy sources not directly derivable from coal. For energy that can be derived from coal such as electric power, the measure is the number of tons of coal required to produce one unit of the related energy source. Electricity generated from nuclear fuels and hydropower is converted to coal equivalents by the heat content of the electric power generated.[1]

The measure most commonly used in India is called the *coal replacement* system. This system was used by the Energy Survey Committee in its 1965 Report and has been used in India in all subsequent work. The coal replacement measure is the amount of coal which would be required to replace other energy sources in use. Because of the different degrees of thermal efficiency with which the alternative energy sources are used in India, a coal replacement measure was considered to be more appropriate than the standard coal equivalent measure used elsewhere. The Report defined the coal replacement measure as follows:

> The 'replacement rations' express the amount of coal needed to substitute for oil products, dung, firewood and waste products in their final use, taking account of the efficiencies involved in typical cases of substitution. The factors for coke and gas are however purely technical conversion factors, permitting the expression of the final consumption of these fuels in terms of the primary input of coal actually needed. The replacement factor used for final electricity consumption permits its expression in terms of the amount of coal that would have been needed if no hydel or oil generation were available.[2]

The factors currently in use for calculating coal replacement and coal equivalent units are provided in Table 2. Although coal replacement factors would change over time with changing efficiency in use of energy sources, the Fuel Policy Committee elected to use the same factors which were calculated by the Energy Survey Committee in the early 1960s. This procedure allows comparison of energy use through time, but the ratios cannot be taken as indicating the coal replacement value for any particular energy source at any given point in time.[3]

To obtain an indication of the relative differences among the three measurement systems, Table 3 displays the shares of energy consumption of major fuels in India in 1970-71. The share of non-commercial energy is highest using the heat content measure and lowest using the coal replacement measure. This difference arises because non-commercial energy sources are generally more inefficient than commercial sources, and this difference in efficiency is taken into account in the coal replacement measure. In other words, the amount of coal equivalent to the heat content of one metric ton of dry dung is much higher than the amount of coal required to replace the dung

1. United Nations, Department of Economic and Social Affairs, *World Energy Supplies 1970-1973*, (Statistical Papers Series J, No. 18), 1975, pp. viii-xiv.
2. Government of India, *Report of the Energy Survey of India Committee*, (New Delhi: Government of India Press, 1965), pp. 10-11.
3. Government of India, *Report of the Fuel Policy Committee*, (Delhi: Government of India Press, 1975), p. 5.

Table 2. Coal equivalent and coal replacement values for selected energy sources.

Energy source	Measurement unit	Coal equivalent (metric tons, mtce)	Coal replacement (metric tons, mtcr)
Coal	1 mt	1.0	1.0
Hard coke	1 mt	1.3	1.3
Soft coke	1 mt	1.5	1.5
Firewood and ag. waste	1 mt	.95	.95
Charcoal	1 mt	1.0	1.0
Dry dung	1 mt		.4
Oil products:			
Black products[a]	1 mt	2.0	2.0
Kerosene and LPG	1 mt	2.0	8.3
HSDO and LDO[b]	1 mt	2.0	9.0
Motor spirit and jet fuel	1 mt	2.0	7.5
Natural Gas	10^9 m^3	1.8	3.6
Electricity	10^9 kwh	1.0	1.0

Sources: G.o.I., *Report of the Fuel Policy Committee*, p. 5, and G.o.I., *Report of the Energy Survey of India Committee*, pp. 10-11.

[a]Fuel oil, furnance oil, refinery fuel, and other such products.
[b]High speed diesel oil and light diesel oil.

for cooking. On the other hand, a much larger amount of coal is required to replace diesel oil (in locomotives, for instance) than is represented by their relative heat contents because diesel engines are more efficient converters of energy.

Table 3. Energy consumption shares for 1970-71 of major fuels using three different measures (percentages).

	Heat content	Coal equivalent	Coal replacement
Commercial energy			
Coal	20.2	16.5	13.6
Oil	12.1	9.8	25.9
Electricity	3.3	15.7	12.8
Total	35.6	42.0	52.2
Non-commercial energy	64.4	58.0	47.8
Total	100.0	100.0	100.0

Source: Dave Henderson, *India, the Energy Sector*, p. 179.

None of the measures of aggregate energy consumption is best for all purposes. Clearly the coal equivalent measure must be used for international comparisons because most of the available data is in this form. For use within India, the coal replacement measure is probably the most suitable because of the important differences among energy sources in efficiency of utilization.

Energy consumption patterns

To compare aggregate consumption data across countries the coal equivalent measure is normally used because most international data is available only in this form. Table 4 displays consumption of commercial energy resources for selected countries in 1973. The selected countries cover a broad range of geographic, political, and economic conditions. Energy consumption per capita in the group of countries ranges from a low of less than fifty kilograms

Table 4. Consumption of commercial energy resources in 1973 for selected countries (metric tons coal equivalent).

Country	*Total Commercial Energy* Aggregate	per capita (1000 kg)	Solid fuels[a]	Liquid fuels[b]	Natural gas	Electricity[c]
USA	2503.2	11.9	508.2	1109.1	839.0	46.9
India	110.4	0.2	78.1	27.7	0.8	3.7
Egypt	10.2	0.3	0.0	9.4	0.1	0.6
Ghana	1.6	0.2	0.0	1.2	0.0	0.4
Brazil	63.4	0.6	4.3	51.0	1.6	6.6
Argentina	47.3	1.9	1.2	34.6	11.1	0.4
Iran	32.9	1.1	1.1	17.1	14.0	0.7
Saudi Arabia	10.3	1.2	0.0	6.1	4.2	0.0
Kuwait	10.9	12.3	0.0	3.9	7.0	0.0
Japan	426.0	3.9	80.7	326.6	7.8	11.0
Thailand	12.7	0.3	0.1	12.3	0.0	0.3
Cambodia	0.2	0.0	0.0	0.2	0.0	0.0
China	463.6	0.6	399.7	55.7	3.9	4.3
France	234.3	4.5	44.3	161.0	21.8	7.3
USSR	1263.2	5.1	470.7	456.3	320.9	15.2
Sweden	48.6	6.0	2.2	38.5	0.0	7.8

Source: United Nations, *World Energy Supplies 1970-1973*, Series *J*, No. 18, pp. 13-35.

[a]Primarily coal.

[b]Primarily petroleum.

[c]Hydropower, nuclear electric power, and imports only. Excludes coal-, petroleum- and natural gas-based generation to avoid double counting.

coal equivalent per person for Cambodia to a high of 12,300 kilograms per person in Kuwait. Energy consumption per capita in India is about two hundred kilograms coal equivalent per year.

Differences among countries in resource reliance can also be determined from Table 4. For example, Kuwait relies exclusively on its domestic oil and natural gas resources. Of course, a portion of these resources is converted to electric power for final consumption. On the other hand, China and India place a much heavier reliance on coal resources. Brazil places a relatively large reliance on hydropower with about 10 percent of its energy consumption being derived from this source.

To place energy consumption patterns in India in perspective, Tables 5 and 6 provide a breakdown of energy consumption in India (Table 5) and the United States (Table 6) by consuming sector and energy source. The Indian data in Table 5 is computed in coal equivalents using conversion factors which are commonly used in India. These factors differ from the factors used by the United Nations, and therefore Table 6 is computed using both the Indian and United Nations factors. Although the sectors are not defined identically in the two countries, comparisons can be made by aggregating some of the Indian sectors. The sum of Indian domestic, agricultural, commercial, and government consumption categories is approximately the same as the United States category, household and commercial. The Indian mining and manufacturing category corresponds to the United States industrial sector, and the transport sectors are essentially the same.[4]

Table 5. Energy consumption in India in 1970-71 by sector and energy source (metric tons coal equivalent and percent).

Sector	Coal		Oil Products		Electricity		Total	
	mtce	%	mtce	%	mtce	%	mtce	%
Mining and manufacturing	31.07	23.9	3.35	2.6	34.35	26.4	68.77	52.9
Transport	15.91	12.3	14.53	11.2	1.43	1.1	31.87	24.5
Domestic	4.07	3.1	8.49	6.5	3.83	3.0	16.39	12.6
Agriculture	0.0	0.0	1.39	1.1	4.54	3.5	5.93	4.6
Commercial government and other	.30	0.2	2.14	1.7	4.50	3.5	6.94	5.3
Total	51.35	39.5	29.90	23.0	48.65	37.5	129.90	100.0

Source: G.o.I., *Report of the Fuel Policy Committee*, p. 130.

4. Ibid., pp. 4-22; and U.S. Department of the Interior, *United States Energy Through the Year 2000* by Walter G. Dupree, Jr., and James A. West, (Washington, D.C.: Government Printing Office, December 1972).

Table 6. Energy consumption in the United States in 1971 by sector and energy source.

Sector	Coal		Petroleum		Natural gas		Electricity		Total	
	mtce	%	mtce	%	mtce	%	mtce	%	mtce	%
U.N. conversion factors:										
Household and Commercial	16.1	0.6	228.4	8.4	268.4	9.9	472.7	17.4	985.6	36.2
Industrial	181.1	6.7	195.1	7.2	381.3	14.0	348.4	12.8	1105.9	40.6
Transport	.3	0.0	597.0	21.9	30.2	1.1	2.7	0.1	630.2	23.2
Total	197.5	7.3	1020.5	37.5	679.9	25.0	823.8	30.3	2721.7	100.0
Indian conversion factors:										
Household and Commercial	16.1	0.4	310.8	7.5	363.2	8.8	926.1	22.5	1616.2	39.2
Industrial	181.1	4.4	265.4	6.4	516.1	12.5	682.6	16.6	1645.2	39.9
Transport	.3	0.0	812.2	19.7	40.9	1.0	5.3	0.1	858.7	20.8
Total	197.5	4.8	1388.4	33.7	920.2	22.3	1614.0	39.2	4120.1	100.0

Sources: Consumption data-U.S. Department of the Interior, *United States Energy Through the Year 2000*, p. 17; U.N. factors-*World Energy Supplies 1970-1973, U.N.* Statistical Series J No. 18, pp. ix-xiii; Indian factors-G.o.I., *Report of the Fuel Policy Committee*, p. 5.

Note: U.N. conversion factors are as follows: coal – 1.0, petroleum – 1.47, natural gas – 1.33 (per 1000 cubic meters), thermal electricity – .6, nuclear and hydropower – .125 (per 1000 kwh). Conversion factors used in India are as follows: coal – 1.0, petroleum – 2.0, natural gas – 1.8, and electricity – 1.0.

As can be seen from Table 6, the major difference which results from the use of Indian conversion factors is that electric power receives a significantly greater weight. The percentage of electric power in total United States consumption changes from 30.3 to 39.2 with the switch from United Nations factors to Indian factors. The United Nations factors are closer to actual heat content values (except for thermal electric power). Using a type of heat content system, the sectoral percentage allocations of United States energy consumption in 1968 were as follows:[5]

Household and commercial	33.6
Industrial	41.2
Transport	25.2

Important differences in energy consumption patterns between the United States and India can be detected by comparing Tables 5 and 6. A significantly greater share of energy is consumed by the industrial sector in India than in the United States. The transport sectors have essentially the same relative share. Household and commercial consumption is significantly lower in India than in the United States (22.5 percent in India versus 36.2 to 39.2 percent in the United States). This difference is caused by two major factors. Domestic demand is smaller due to lower incomes and standard of living. Rural consumption is lower, relatively, because of the lack of rural electrification and the large percentage of non-commercial energy consumption in rural India.

Looking at the individual energy resources, coal is clearly much more important in India than in the United States. Heavy energy intensive industry such as steel production consumes large amounts of coal, and is a larger share of the total industrial sector in India than in the United States. This has resulted from the deliberate effort to build an industrial sector in India emphasizing heavy industry. The transport sector in India also consumes a much greater proportion of coal than in the United States because much of the railway transport is steam (coal) powered. Very little natural gas is consumed in India, yet the direct consumption of natural gas in the United States amounts to about one-fourth of total energy consumption. In addition, about four trillion cubic feet of natural gas were consumed in electric power generation in 1971.[6]

5. Stanford Research Institute, *Patterns of Energy Consumption in the United States*, Report to the U.S. Office of Science and Technology, (Washington, D.C.: Government Printing Office, January 1972), p. 6.
6. U.S. Department of the Interior, *United States Energy*, p. 17.

Electric power is relatively more important in the industrial sector in India than in the United States. This difference is caused primarily by the ready availability of cheaper (at least in the past), more efficient alternatives – oil and natural gas – in the United States. Household and commercial electric power consumption is about twice as important, relatively, in the United States as in India.

This review of energy consumption patterns provides background for the analysis of resource endowments in India. By comparing consumption patterns in India with those of the United States and other countries, it is easier to place the current energy resource situation in India in perspective.

COAL

Coal is a fuel of vegetable origin which comes in a variety of forms. Ranked in ascending order of BTU content, the lowest form of coal is lignite, and the highest form is anthracite. Bituminous coal falls in between these two forms. Table 7 lists the average chemical properties of these types of coal and of peat, a precursor of coal. Bituminous coal covers the range between lignite and anthracite. The six grades of bituminous coal are sub-bituminous; low, medium, and high rank bituminous; and low and high rank semi-bituminous. Coke, which is used in steel manufacturing, is coal with the volatile components removed. It is often produced from high grades of bituminous coal.[7]

Estimates of coal resources vary significantly by source of estimate and especially through time. For example, in 1922, the Geological Survey of India estimated coal reserves at 25.6 billion tons of which only five billion tons were considered proved reserves.[8] In 1972, the GSI estimated total coal reserves at eighty-one billion tons of which 21.4 billion tons were considered proved reserves.[9]

In the coal classification scheme used in India, *proved reserves* are classified as those within two hundred meters of existing workings, outcrops or boreholes. *Indicated reserves* are those for which observation points are available no more than one thousand meters apart, or two thousand meters for beds of known continuity. *Inferred reserves* are those based upon general

7. G.S. Singh, *Economic and Commercial Geography*, (Bombay: P.C. Manaktala and Sons Private, Ltd., 1967), pp. 99-100.
8. Dagli, p. 186.
9. Geological Survey of India, *GSI News*, Vol. 3, No. 4, (Calcutta: *GSI* Press, April 1972), pp. 6-7.

Table 7. Average properties of coal-fuels (in percentage).

Type	Moisture	Volatile matter	Carbon	Ash	Approximate composition of dried samples excluding water and ash			Heat value in BTU per lb.
					Carbon	Hydrogen	Oxygen	
Peat	15.0	50.0	25.0	10.0	59.0	5.0	36.0	4,500
Lignite	32.0	30.0	29.0	9.0	67.0	6.0	27.0	6,500
Bituminous coal[a]	4.0	35.0	53.0	8.0	80.0	5.0	15.0	14,000
Anthracite	3.3	3.0	91.0	2.7	95.0	2.5	2.5	15,500

Source: Singh, *Economic and Commercial Geography*, p. 99.

[a]Sub-bituminous coals range from 7000 to about 12,000 BTU per pound.

knowledge of the coal beds even though there are no observation points within one or two thousand meters.[10]

In 1972, the Geological Survey of India provided new estimates of reserves in place using this classification scheme. Reserve estimates by state for coking coal, non-coking coal, and lignite are shown in Table 8. Of the total reserves in place, only a portion are recoverable and usable as coal products. For non-coking coal, only about 75 percent of the reserves in place have an ash content of less than 40 percent which means that one-fourth of the coal in place is not economically or technically usable. Furthermore, not all of the reserves in place can actually be mined. An average recovery factor for Indian coal in place is about 55 percent for non-coking coal. Therefore, only 41 percent of the non-coking coal in place is actually recoverable and usable ($.75 \times .55 = .41$). For coking coal, losses occur not only in mining but also in washing (to remove ash) such that only about 29 percent of the coking coal in place is actually recoverable and usable.[11] Using these factors, the total recoverable reserves of non-coking coal become 25 billion metric tons and the recoverable reserves of coking coal become 5.8 billion metric tons. Of this, only 1.6 billion metric tons is prime coking coal with the remainder being medium and blendable coking coals. Excluding lignite, the total recoverable coal reserves of India are 30.9 billion metric tons.

10. Geological Survey of India Officers, *Coal Resources of India*, Vol. 88, (Calcutta: Pooran Press, 1971), pp. 488-89.
11. P. D. Henderson, *India: The Energy Sector*, (Washington, D.C.: World Bank, 1975), pp. 6-8.

Table 8. Coal reserves of India (million tons).

	Proved	Indicated	Inferred	Total
Non-coking coal:				
West Bengal	3071.6	5219.8	8847.3	17138.6
Bihar	2603.7	8648.8	6612.3	17864.8
Madhya Pradesh	4140.9	3863.8	7168.4	15173.1
Orissa	895.4	2411.0	1810.1	5116.5
Maharashtra	477.9	799.7	1344.1	2621.7
Andhra Pradesh	978.0	1077.2	0.0	2055.1
Assam, Meghalaya, Arunachal and Nagaland[a]	139.0	290.6	398.0	827.6
Total non-coking coal:	12306.5	22310.9	26180.2	60797.4
Coking coal:				
West Bengal	966.8	775.1	738.4	2480.3
– medium	388.1	296.7	200.9	855.7
– semi and weakly	578.7	478.4	537.5	1594.6
Bihar	7986.6	7469.5	1909.3	17365.4
– prime	3653.2	1537.3	460.7	5651.2
– medium	3393.8	3820.0	1071.3	8285.1
– semi and weakly	939.6	2112.2	377.3	3429.1
Madhya Pradesh	105.7	203.7	0.0	309.4
– medium	69.5	193.3	0.0	262.8
– semi and weakly	36.2	10.4	0.0	46.6
Total coking coal:	9059.1	8448.3	2647.7	20155.1
– prime	3653.2	1537.3	460.7	5651.2
– medium	3851.4	4310.0	1272.2	9433.6
– semi and weakly	1554.5	2601.0	914.8	5070.3
Total coal[b]	21365.6	30759.2	28827.9	80952.5
Lignite:				
Tamil Nadu	1717.0	202.0	0.0	1919.0
Gujarat	151.6	0.0	0.0	151.6
Jammu and Kashmir	0.0	0.0	8.4	8.4
Rajasthan	0.0	0.0	20.3	20.3
Total lignite:	1868.6	202.0	28.7	2099.3

Source: Geological Survey of India News, April 1972.

Note: These estimates include only coal in seams 1.2 meters (4 feet) and above in thickness and up to 609 meters (2000 feet) in depth.

[a]tertiary coal

[b]excluding lignite

These resource estimates are based only on the coal in place to a depth not exceeding two thousand feet, and, of course, they do not include potential future upward revisions in the coal reserve estimates. According to current estimates of demand, the coking coal resources should be adequate for about forty years.[12] Non-coking coal resources may be adequate for sixty-five to four hundred years depending on the consumption projections that are utilized. If 1974-1975 production is rounded to ninety million tons and annual production is assumed to grow at a 3 percent rate (but not allowed to exceed six hundred million tons/year), the non-coking coal resources would last about eighty years. Since these consumption growth assumptions are rather optimistic, and the reserve base will likely expand with time, the eighty year exhaustion period should be considered a minimum.

To gain a better perspective on the Indian coal reserve situation, India's resources may be compared with those of other world countries. India has about 0.8 percent of the world's total coal resources, and in 1971 India produced 2.4 percent of total world coal production. The United States has about 27.2 percent of total world resources, and it accounted for 16.7 percent of world production in 1971. Similarly, Japan has about 0.1 percent of world resources but produced 1.1 percent of all coal in 1971.[13] Coal reserve and production data for a number of countries and regions are provided in Table 9. Compared to most world countries, India is relatively well endowed with coal resources.

OIL AND NATURAL GAS

The first commercial oil discovery in India was made in Assam in 1867, just eight years after the Drake discovery in the United States.[14] Since that time, exploration and development of petroleum in India has proceeded at a very slow pace relative to other areas of the world. A number of authors have placed much of the blame for lack of development of India's petroleum sector since independence on the international oil companies.[15] At this point, how-

12. Kirit Parikh, *Second India Studies: Energy*, (Delhi: McMillan Co. of India, Ltd., 1976), p. 38.
13. World Energy Conference, *Survey of Energy Resources*, (New York: The U.S. National Committee of the World Energy Conference, 1974), pp. 31-65.
14. M. R. Chaudhuri, *Power Resources of India*, (Calcutta: Oxford and I.B.H. Publishing Co., 1970), pp. 38-42.
15. With somewhat different approaches and conclusions, three such studies are: (1) Biplab Dasgupta, *The Oil Industry in India* (London: Frank Cass and Co., Ltd., 1971); (2) H. Lal, *Indian Petroleum* (New Delhi: Delhi Press for Lifeline Publications, 1963); (3) Michael Tanzer, *The Political Economy of International Oil and the Underdeveloped Countries* (Boston: Beacon Press, 1969).

ever, we are only interested in the current resource situation of oil and natural gas and projections for future petroleum resource development.

The proved reserves of petroleum in India are rather sparse compared with the coal reserves. As of 1972, proved and indicated reserves amounted to about 128 million tons (970 million barrels) of oil and about 62.5 billion cubic meters (2.2 trillion cubic feet) of natural gas.[16] However, since the recent discovery of a major oil field at Bombay High and another discovery nearby on the Bassein structure, proved oil reserves in India are currently estimated at about 400 million tons (3 billion barrels). The approximate breakdown of these reserves is as follows:

Bombay High	200 million tons
Bassein	75 million tons
Proven onshore reserves	125 million tons

Natural gas reserves are estimated to have increased from 62.4 billion cubic meters to greater than 100 billion cubic meters. Hence, in four years proven oil reserves in India have increased by over 200 percent and natural gas reserves have almost doubled.[17]

In addition, the potential for future petroleum discoveries in parts of India is quite good. Oil is found in areas of sedimentary deposits of past ages. The

Table 9. Coal reserves and production of selected countries and regions.

Country	Reserves (million tons)	Percent of world reserves	Production (thousand tons)	Percent of world production 1971
USA	2,924,503	27.2	509,930	16.7
USSR	5,713,600	53.1	694,000	22.7
China, PR of	1,000,000	9.3	410,000	13.5
Europe	607,521	5.7	1,117,680	36.4
India	82,977	0.8	72,820	2.4
South Africa	44,339	0.4	58,520	1.9
Japan	8,628	0.1	34,110	1.1
Turkey	7,282	0.1	10,000	0.3
Latin America	32,928	0.3	10,980	0.4

Source: World Energy Conference, *Survey of Energy Resources*, pp. 31-65.

16. Parikh, *Energy*, p. 39.
17. Larry Auldridge, 'India Steps Up Exploration, Development.' *Oil and Gas Journal*, (August 23, 1976): p. 52.

total sedimentary area of India is about 1.67 million square kilometers including about 40 percent of the land area of India, and 380 thousand square kilometers of potential oil producing area offshore (up to a water depth of 200 meters). Historically, in the rest of the world, only about 3 percent of the sedimentary areas has been found to contain petroleum. Of the total potential oil bearing areas (offshore and onshore) in India, about 300,000 square kilometers (18 percent of the total sedimentary area) are considered to be good prospects. Another 15 percent of the sedimentary area is considered to have medium prospects and the remainder is assessed as having fair or low petroleum potential.[18] Recently,a team of Soviet and Indian experts assessed the country's oil potential at about 5900 million metric tons (45 billion barrels). Natural gas potential was fixed at 7500 billion cubic meters (265 trillion cubic feet). Almost 70 percent of this potential oil and natural gas is offshore, and only about 15 percent of the offshore sedimentary area has been explored.[19] A significant opportunity exists for future petroleum finds especially in the offshore areas. The importance of this potential in current and future energy supply development policy will be explored in Chapter 4.

It is interesting to compare India's oil situation with that of other world countries. In 1975, the United States Geological Survey estimated that the undiscovered oil resources of the United States may range from 6600 to 16,760 million metric tons (50-127 billion barrels). A number of other estimates have fallen in this range.[20] If the Indian estimate of 5900 million metric tons was done on a comparable basis, the comparison indicates that India may be in a relatively good position in the future if the potential is realized. Table 10 provides data on proven oil reserves and 1972 oil production for a selected group of countries and regions. Clearly, India is unlikely to discover reserves to match countries such as Iran and Saudi Arabia, but she may be able to discover enough oil to meet much of her domestic requirement.

HYDROPOWER

Between the years 1953 and 1958, the Central Water and Power Commission conducted an extensive survey of the hydro-electric potential of India. The study was based on specific schemes of development which could be used in

18. G.o.I., *Fuel Policy Committee*, p. 25.
19. Auldridge, p. 52.
20. Robert J. Kalter, Wallace E. Tyner, and Daniel W. Hughes, *Alternative Energy Leasing Strategies and Schedules for the Outer Continental Shelf* (Ithaca: Agriculture Economics Research Series 75-33, Cornell University, 1975), p. 9.

Table 10. Oil reserves and production of selected countries and regions.

Country	Reserves[a] (million tons)	Percent of world reserves[a]	1972 Production (million tons)
USA	5569.0	6.1	436.2
USSR	8318.0	9.1	394.0
Europe	1394.0	1.5	35.4
India[b]	127.8	0.1	7.4
Iran	8870.0	9.7	255.4
Indonesia	1456.0	1.6	53.2
Malaysia	194.6	0.2	4.5
Saudi Arabia	18727.0	20.5	300.7
Peru	101.1	0.1	3.0
Venezuela	6093.0	6.7	168.3

Sources: World Energy Conference, *Survey of Energy Resources*, pp. 108-110; and G.o.I., *Report of the Fuel Policy Committee*, p. 26.

[a]Proved recoverable oil reserves.
[b]As of 1976, proved recoverable oil reserves in India are about 400 million metric tons.

future planning rather than on a theoretical analysis of the hydropower potential. It was felt that this approach would be more realistic and would provide data useful for other aspects of planning such as determining the physical location of power plants. The study concluded that 41.16 million kilowatts is the economically utilizable hydropower capacity available to India from its river systems. At a 60 percent load factor, this corresponds to 216 terawatt hours (billion kilowatt hours) annual output.[21]

Table 11 provides the regional breakdown of hydropower resources and the level and percentage of development in each region. Only 17.5 percent of India's hydropower resources has been developed to date.[22] Comparing Tables 11 and 8 it is clear that India's hydropower resources are distributed much more evenly than her coal resources. In most parts of India, a significant amount of hydropower potential remains to be tapped.

The 41 million kilowatt capacity should be viewed as a very conservative estimate. The relative prices of alternative energy sources have increased dramatically since the original study, meaning that more hydropower projects would now be economical than before. In addition, technology in hydropower generation has improved considerably over the twenty years since this study was undertaken. Also, the potential of India and Nepal jointly developing the Karnali River Valley in Nepal which was excluded from the original study has increased considerably since the early 1960s. For these and

21. G.o.I., *Energy Survey Committee*, pp. 185-92.
22. G.o.I., *Fuel Policy Committee*, p. 28.

Table 11. Regional distribution of hydropower potential and development.

Region	Hydropower resources (mw)	Developed hydropower (mw)	Percentage developed (%)
Southern	8,097	3,221	38.8
Western	7,189	942	13.1
Northern	10,731	2,451	22.8
Eastern	2,694	475	21.3
North-Eastern	12,464	38	0.3
Total	41,155	7,225	17.5

Source: G.o.I., *Report of the Fuel Policy Committee*, p. 28.

other reasons, a current conservative estimate of the hydropower potential of India is about 50 million kilowatts.[23] Clearly, the potential for expanding the hydropower energy source is enormous. The importance of this potential for future energy policy will be discussed further in Chapter 5.

In addition to looking at the total and regional potential for hydropower, it is also interesting to see the breakdown of this potential by type of hydropower. Table 12 displays the breakdown of potential hydropower by type. Of this total potential power capacity, only 41.2 million kilowatts were considered to be available to India since the remainder is from river basins primarily in Nepal. Note that over half of the total power potential is in the medium and high head projects. For these and other projects, only prime power was estimated. In other words, when flows are larger, significant amounts of secondary power would be available from these systems.

Table 12. Hydropower capacity by type of project.

	Type of project	Capacity (million kw)	Percent
1.	Run of the river	10.3	20.0
2.	Low head (drops of 8-30 meters)	3.7	7.1
3.	Medium head (drops of 30-300 meters)	23.9	46.4
4.	High head (drops of over 300 meters)	13.6	26.5
		50.5	100.0

Source: G.o.I., *Report of the Energy Survey Committee*, p. 192.

23. Henderson, p. 18.

India ranks seventh among world countries in potential hydropower resources just behind the United States. Hydropower potential may be ranked by the average energy producible (at partial load) throughout the year (G_a) or by the energy producible 95 percent of the time (G_{95}). Most hydropower facilities operate in the range between G_a and G_{95}.[24] Table 13 provides hydropower resource estimates for selected countries using both G_a and G_{95} measures.

NUCLEAR ENERGY RESOURCES

Currently, the major nuclear fuel resource used in India is uranium. The major concentration of uranium ores is in Bihar state. The estimated proved reserve of uranium ore is 3.5 million tons which can be converted to about 22,000 tons of U_3O_8. In addition, inferred reserves amount to about 24,000 tons of U_3O_8.[25] Almost all these resources are high cost resources as India has negligible quantities of low cost (below $26/kilogram of uranium) uranium reserves. These resources could be rapidly depleted if construction of nuclear power generation facilities advanced significantly in India.

For the longer term, India is richly endowed with reserves of thorium which can be used as a fuel in the breeder reactors now being developed. India's

Table 13. Hydropower resources of selected countries.

Country	G_a		G_{95}	
	Power generation (Gwh/yr.)	Capacity (mw)	Power generation (Gwh/yr.)	Capacity (mw)
USA	701,500	186,700	216,100	27,000
USSR	1,095,000	269,000	400,000	50,000
China, PR of	1,320,000	330,000	480,000	60,000
India	280,000	70,000	216,600	27,100
Zaire	660,000	132,000	620,800	77,600
Brazil	519,300	90,200	382,500	47,800
Peru	109,200	12,500	30,700	3,800
Mexico	99,400	20,300	85,100	10,600

Source: World Energy Conference, *Survey of Energy Resources*, p. 173.

24. World Energy Conference, pp. 161-63.
25. G.o.I., *Fuel Policy Committee*, pp. 28-29.

450,000 tons of thorium constitute the world's largest reserves. The United States has approximately 300,000 tons of thorium reserves. Together, the two countries have almost half of the world's thorium reserves.[26] Much of India's resource is located in the state of Kerala.

If a breeder reactor technology comes on line which can utilize thorium, India would have enough of this resource to last for hundreds of years. Scientists and planners in India hope that this technology will be developed by the late 1980s. However, the process is likely to take much longer and may not be developed to the point of widespread commercial application in India before the year 2000. The timing depends not only on research and development investment and progress in India but also on the pace of technology development in the West, where thorium may not be the major fuel for breeder reactors.

NON-COMMERCIAL ENERGY SOURCES

Non-commercial energy resources in India consist primarily of firewood, cow dung, and vegetable waste. These non-commercial energy sources account for at least half of the total energy consumption in India (the actual proportion depending on how energy consumption is measured – see Table 3). The Fuel Policy Committee estimated that 123 million tons of firewood and charcoal, 67 million tons of dung cakes, and 38 million tons of vegetable waste were consumed as energy in 1970-71. In terms of coal replacement, these amounts were equivalent to 117, 27 and 36 million tons of coal respectively.[27]

In terms of coal replacement, the share of non-commercial sources fell from 60 percent in 1960-61 to 48 percent in 1970-71. In fact, as one might expect, the share has fallen consistently since the first statistics were gathered in 1953-54.[28]

Just as the statistics on consumption of non-commercial energy are considered to be subject to a high degree of error, the resource base is also known for its high degree of inaccuracy. For example, India has about 75 million hectares of forest land of which about 60 million hectares is considered to be potentially useful (commercial forest land, in U.S. terminology). Almost all of this forest land is owned by the state governments. For the year 1969-70, the recorded fuelwood harvest from the state forests amounted to only 9 million tons out of the 130 million tons of estimated annual consumption.

26. World Energy Conference, p. 214.
27. G.o.I., *Fuel Policy Committee*, p. 9.
28. Ibid., and G.o.I., *Energy Survey Committee*, pp. 11-12.

Consequently, the recorded production amounted to only about 7 percent of total estimated consumption. The remainder of the consumption must have come from one of three sources:

- production from forest land not owned by the states
- unrecorded production from state forest lands
- production from village lands or roadsides not officially designated as forest lands[29]

Whatever the source, it is clear that the current consumption is much beyond the maximum sustainable yield, and that India's forest lands are being depleted. The problem has been recognized and is now being studied by planners in India.

The other non-commercial energy sources in India, cow dung and vegetable wastes, are renewable resources in the sense that so long as draft animals are employed in production and crops are produced, these energy sources will be produced as by-products. However, the cow dung has an alternative use as a fertilizer for crop production. Some of the vegetable waste could also be used as animal feed. It has been proposed that these resources be used as raw materials for generating biogas (methane gas) at the village or farm level to provide for more efficient energy conversion of the resources than at present.[30] Used in this manner, the potential energy has been estimated at 100 million tons of coal replacement per year.[31] This possibility will be discussed in more detail in Chapter 6. Non-commercial energy sources and potential uses of these raw materials must form an important part of energy policy for a country with an energy consumption pattern such as that in India.

OTHER ENERGY SOURCES

Solar energy

Solar energy is considered to be of considerable importance for the future energy supply picture in India. The potential was summarized by Kirit Parikh as follows:

29. Henderson, p. 30.
30. Parikh, *Energy*; Arjun Makhijani with Alan Poole, *Energy and Agriculture in the Third World* (Cambridge: Ballinger Publishing Co. for the Ford Foundation, 1975); C. R. Prasad, K. Krishna Prasad, and A. K. N. Reddy, 'Bio-Gas Plants: Prospects, Problems and Tasks.' *Economic and Political Weekly* Special Number (August 1974): pp. 1347-64; and M. A. Sathianathan, *Bio-Gas Achievements and Challenges*, (New Delhi: Universal Book Co., 1975).
31. Parikh, *Energy*, p. 46.

A large amount of solar radiation falls in India, and for most of the country, very few days are without sunshine. The annual average intensity of solar radiation in India is 600 calories per square centimeter per day.... even the minimum available radiation in the month of December is also quite large, and for most cities, it is above 500 calories/cms^2/day. Thus, solar energy is an attractive source of energy for India.[32]

By contrast, the highest average intensity of solar radiation in the United States (in the West-south central region) is 430 calories per square centimeter.[33] The January average for this region is 260 calories per square centimeter. Hence, India receives much more solar radiation than even the highest region of the United States. Progress in the development of solar energy technology in India will be discussed in Chapter 6.

Alternative energy sources

A number of alternative energy sources are being considered in India. Among these are wind power, tidal energy, geothermal energy, and chemical energy sources. At this point and for the near future, none of these resources is expected to make a significant contribution to India's energy supply.[34]

SUMMARY

In conclusion, several important points are evident from the preceding information:

1. Energy policy in India cannot ignore the proportion on non-commercial energy which is consumed. Future energy consumption patterns are at the core of the formation of sound energy policy. Influencing these patterns could be a key factor in stimulating future economic growth and development, especially in the rural sector.
2. India is well endowed with non-coking coal for the near term with sufficient resources to last at least eighty years.
3. Most of the hydropower potential in India is yet to be developed. This resource could contribute in a major way to long term energy supply development in India.

32. Ibid., p. 42.
33. Federal Energy Administration, *Project Independence Blueprint Final Task Force Report-Solar Energy* (Washington, D.C., 1974), p. A-I-9.
34. G.o.I., *Fuel Policy Committee*, pp. 29-31.

4. Thorium, as a nuclear (breeder reactor) feed stock, has tremendous potential in the long term, but not for at least twenty years. In the short term, India will have to rely on other resources.
5. The biggest unknown in the Indian resource picture is oil and natural gas. Very little exploration has been conducted in the past although the pace has quickened within the last two years. With adequate exploration and development, India could possibly become self-sufficient in oil.
6. Of all the alternative energy sources, only solar energy and biogas generation offer any potential for large scale development in the near future.

The implications of these points for future energy policy will be examined in more detail in subsequent chapters.

3. Energy resource development in the five year plans

Energy resource development is not considered as a unified topic in any of the five year plans. In addition, the grouping of energy investments changed from plan to plan reflecting changes in administrative organization. The earlier plans contain a section on irrigation and power which covers investments in hydropower and thermal power plants. The Fourth and Fifth Plans separate irrigation and flood control from power investments. Coal resource development is discussed under the heading of mineral resource development. Oil and natural gas resource investments are covered under industrial development, or a similar classification, and investments in nuclear energy are included in scientific, technical, and industrial research or the power category. Throughout the planning period, each energy resource was considered together with the use for that energy or as a part of the industrial or development sector to which it was attached. In the material that follows, an effort will be made to separate energy resource investments from the development sector to which they are attached for planning purposes and to recombine them in such a way as to obtain an overall picture of energy resource development strategies over the five year plans.

Between the Third and Fourth Plans, three annual plans were utilized by the Government of India. These plans will not be discussed here because they essentially consisted of completing projects undertaken in the Third Plan, or amounted to an extension of the direction provided by the Third Plan.

ELECTRIC POWER

First Five Year Plan (1951-1956)

In the First Five Year Plan a total of Rs. 558 crores (one crore equals ten million) was allocated to electric power development and irrigation. Of this amount, Rs. 518 crores was allocated to completion of the projects (mostly multipurpose) under construction. In addition to providing somewhat over one million kilowatts of electric power these projects were expected to increase irrigated acreage by 8.5 million acres during the First Plan, and ultimately by 16.9 million acres. The remaining Rs. 40 crores of expenditures on electric power development in the First Plan was allocated to development work on five new projects to be initiated in the last two years of the plan. Total cost of these projects was expected to exceed Rs. 200 crores.[1]

Second Five Year Plan (1956-1961)

The total planned outlay for power development in the Second Plan was Rs. 427 crores.[2] This investment was expected to yield 3.5 million kilowatts of additional power generating capacity in the Second Plan period. The emphasis in new generating capacity in the Second Plan was in hydropower although a significant amount of new thermal (coal) power was planned and a very small amount of diesel generation also included. The Second Plan also called for power load surveys to be undertaken during the first three years of the plan. These surveys were considered important for future planning efforts because of the increasing rate of change in electricity demand during the First Plan.[3]

Third Five Year Plan (1961-1966)

Electric generating capacity increased from 2.3 million kilowatts at the beginning of the First Plan to 5.7 million kilowatts at the beginning of the Third Plan. During the Second Plan, the average annual increase in generating capacity was about .45 million kilowatts. During the Third Plan it was hoped to increase this rate threefold to an average annual rate of 1.4 million kilowatts raising total installed capacity to 12.7 million kilowatts at the end of the plan period.

The total investment in the Third Plan for electric power generation and distribution was planned at Rs. 1089 crores of which Rs. 1039 crores was to be in the public sector. The breakdown of this proposed expenditure is provided in Table 14. The Third Plan also called for intensive examination and in-

1. Government of India, *First Five Year Plan* (Delhi: Government of India Publications Branch, 1953), p. 157.
2. In the Second Plan, power development was separated from irrigation. The Second Plan indicates that Rs. 260 crores (of the total of Rs. 558 crores) of the combined First Plan expenditure should be allocated to power development alone (*Second Plan*, p. 334).
3. Government of India, Planning Commission, *Second Five Year Plan* (Delhi: Government of India, 1956), pp. 331-71.

vestigation of the remaining hydropower potential in India. Hydropower projects require long lead times and the Plan aimed at advancing some of the preliminary planning for potential future projects. The Plan also called for research on generation, transmission, and distribution problems at the Power Research Institute in Bangalore.[4]

Table 14. Third Plan expenditures for electric power generation and distribution.

Item	Amount (Rs. in crores)
Power generation (hydro and thermal)	661
Atomic power	51
Transmission and distribution (incl. Rs. 105 crores for rural electrification)	327
Total	1039

Source: G.o.I., *Third Five Year Plan Summary*, pp. 108-09.

Fourth Five Year Plan (1969-1974)

During the Third Plan and the three annual plans electricity generating capacity grew at annual rates of 12.5 percent and 12.6 percent respectively. During the Fourth Plan period, capacity was to be increased from 14.29 to 23.00 million kilowatts, a growth rate slightly less than 10 percent. Planned investment for power generation in the public sector during the Fourth Plan was Rs. 2447.57 crores. The distribution of this investment is given in Table 15.

Note that the accounting in the Fourth Plan included not only allocations by the central government but also investment by the state governments. The central government investment of Rs. 210 crores on continuing schemes included Rs. 120 crores on atomic power generation, Rs. 49.25 crores on the Badarpur thermal station, Rs. 38.85 crores for thermal stations at Chandrapura, and Rs. 2 crores on the Neyveli thermal station. New investment by the central government included the Loktak hydroelectric project in Manipur, the Baira-Siul hydroelectric project in Himachal Pradesh and Salal hydroelectric project in Jammu and Kashmir. In total, 9.26 million kilowatts of generating capacity was planned for the Fourth Plan period. In addition,

4. Government of India, Planning Commission, *Third Five Year Plan Summary* (Delhi: Government of India Publications Division, 1962), pp. 108-11.

Table 15. Outlay for power during the Fourth Plan.

Item	States	Union territories	Centre	Centrally sponsored	Total
Generation	974.06	25.48	255.10	—	1254.64
continuing schemes	823.82	25.00	210.10	—	1058.92
new schemes	150.24	0.48	45.00	—	195.72
Transmission and distribution	645.51	44.27	9.80	22.00	721.58
Rural electrification	285.15	9.54	150.00	—	444.69
Investigation and miscellaneous	14.35	2.49	9.82	—	26.66
Total	1919.07	81.78	424.72	22.00	2447.57

Source: G.o.I., *Fourth Five Year Plan 1969-74*, p. 269.

the program for conducting pre-investment surveys of potential hydroelectric sights was continued during the Fourth Plan.[5]

Summary of first four plans

Investment in power development has steadily increased through the four five year plans. Table 16 provides a summary of the investment over the five year plans. Investment in power has grown both as a percent of planned investment and proportion of actual public sector expenditure.

From 1951 through 1974 installed electric generating capacity grew at an average rate of about 9.2 percent. During the first three plans, capacity grew at a 10.8 percent rate. Statistics on the growth in generating capacity over this period are provided in Table 17. As of 1974, India's generating capacity was 60 percent thermal (mostly coal), 37 percent hydropower, and 3 percent nuclear.

Progress in increasing electric generating capacity has consistently fallen behind schedule during the entire planning period. The shortfall was particularly significant during the Fourth Plan when only one-half of the planned additions were completed. Table 18 shows the planned increases, actual achievements, and percentage shortfall for each of the plan periods.

5. Government of India, Planning Commission, *Fourth Five Year Plan 1969-74* (Delhi: Government of India Publications Branch, 1970), pp. 266-73.

Table 16. Expenditure on power development during the plans.

Plan period	Generation		Distribution and transmission		Rural electrification		Total		% of Plan investment	% of Total public sector expenditure
	Planned	Actual	Planned	Actual	Planned	Actual	Planned	Actual		(Actual)
I Plan		159		113		30	260	302	13	7.6
II Plan	235	272	117	178	75	75	427	525	9	9.7
III Plan	712	950	222	308	105	125	1039	1383	13	14.6
Annual Plans	644	718		246		180		1144		14.5
IV Plan	1255	1555	722	806	445	568	2448[a]	2983	15.4	17.5

Source: Venkataraman, *Power Development in India*, pp. 6-9; Lakshmanan, *Economic Development in India*, pp. 1-29; plus First, Second, Third, Fourth, and Fifth Five Year Plans (sections on Power).

[a]Totals do not sum because of a small allocation for miscellaneous items.

Table 17. Growth of installed capacity by type of plant (million kilowatts).

Capacity	1960-61	1965-66	1968-69	1973-74
Installed capacity	5.65	10.17	14.29	18.87
Hydro	1.92	4.10	5.91	6.96
Thermal	3.40	5.65	7.88	11.33[a]
Diesel	0.33	0.42	0.50	—
Nuclear	—	—	—	.58

Sources: G.o.I., *Fourth Plan*, p. 267; G.o.I., *Fifth Plan*, p. 120.

[a]Includes both thermal (coal fired) and diesel.

Table 18. Planned and actual increases in installed generating capacity 1951-1974.

	Plan	Installed generating capacity (million kw)				Percentage shortfall
		Cumulative		Additions		
		Planned	Actual	Planned	Actual	
1.	First Plan (1951-56)	3.60	3.40	1.30	1.10	15
2.	Second Plan (1956-61)	6.90	5.65	3.50	2.25	36
3.	Third Plan (1961-66)	12.69	10.17	7.04	4.52	36
4.	Annual Plans (1966-69)	15.60	14.29	5.43	4.12	24
5.	Fourth Plan (1969-74)	23.00	18.87	9.26	4.58	50

Source: G.o.I., *Fifth Five Year Plan*, p. 118.

Fifth Five Year Plan (1974-79)

During the Fifth Five Year Plan, the planned electric power capacity additions are 16.5 million kilowatts. This increase would amount to a 12 percent annual growth rate in capacity. The breakdown of this planned increase is provided in Table 19. This capacity addition is expected to cost Rs. 6190 crores. The allocation of planned financial expenditures is provided in Table 20. Note that 88 percent of the total investment is the responsibility of the states and union territories. Although the Fifth Plan calls for significant increases in power generating capacity, two-thirds of this increase is required to compensate for shortfalls experienced in earlier plans.[6]

6. Government of India, Planning Commission, *Draft Fifth Five Year Plan 1974-79*, 2 vols. (New Delhi: Government of India Press, Vol. I-1973, Vol. II-1974), 2: 117-26.

Table 19. Planned generating capacity additions during the Fifth Plan (million kilowatts).

Item	Hydropower	Thermal	Nuclear	Total
Utilities				
1. carry-over projects	5.54	4.49	.71	10.74
2. new projects	.88	4.71		5.59
Non-utilities		.22		.22
Total	6.42	9.42	.71	16.55

Source: G.o.I., *Fifth Five Year Plan*, p. 120.

Table 20. Planned expenditures for power during the Fifth Plan (Rs. crores).

Item	States	Union territories	Center	Total
1. Generation	2765.8	15.0	543.0	3323.8
a. carry-over projects	984.7		241.9	1226.6
b. new projects	1781.2	15.0	301.1	2097.3
2. Transmission and distribution	1429.8	74.5	130.0	1634.3
3. Rural electrification	1079.6	18.7		1098.2
4. Miscellaneous	67.4	1.6	64.8	133.7
Total[a]	5342.6	109.7	737.7	6190.0

Source: G.o.I., *Fifth Five Year Plan*, p. 119.

[a]Totals may not sum due to rounding.

COAL

First Five Year Plan

With respect to coal, the emphasis of the First Plan was in two general areas. First, an effort was to be made to determine the quantity and quality of coal resources available in India. A coal classification scheme suitable for India based on caloric value, ash and moisture content, and coking property was to be established. Although coal reserves in general were considered to be fairly adequate, the reserves of coking coal, essential in the production of steel, were believed to be in short supply. As its second area of emphasis, the Planning Commission recommended legislation to enforce conservation of high-grade coking coal. Nonessential uses of this resource were to be limited (such as by the railways which then consumed 40 percent of the coking coal), and an additional excise tax was placed on coke to further encourage reduced consumption.[7]

Second Five Year Plan

Increased coal production received first priority in the development of mineral resources in the Second Plan. Total coal output in 1955 in India was 38 million tons of which 4.5 million tons was produced in the public sector. The estimated demand at the end of the Second Five Year Plan was 60 million tons. Of the additional 22 million tons needed annually by 1960, 12 million tons was projected to come from the public sector, almost a threefold increase. The plan estimated that a total of about Rs. 60 crores would be needed to achieve the 12 million tons of incremental output in the public sector. Initially, Rs. 40 crores was allocated to the effort. Because of the difficulties of transporting coal from the eastern coal fields over great distances to the markets, about half the new output was to be obtained from fields in outlying areas. For example, the Korba field was to be opened in Madhya Pradesh and was expected to produce 4 million tons by 1960-61. Also, output in the Sasti field in Madhya Pradesh was to be expanded by 3 million tons. Output was also to be increased in the Singareni field near Hyderabad. Nonetheless, about 45 million tons of coal, or three-fourths of the total output would still come from the eastern states of West Bengal and Bihar in 1960-61.

At the beginning of the Second Plan, the supply and consumption of coking coal was still a major problem. Limiting the nonessential uses of coking coal had not been achieved. In 1955, production of coking coal was 14 million tons of which only 3.5 million tons was considered to be for essential uses. The remainder was consumed by the railways and small industries. The railways, however, had agreed to a plan for the phased reduction in their use of coking coal.

The Second Plan also provided Rs. 6 crores to establish coal washeries to improve the quality of coking coal for steel production. In addition, private collieries were encouraged to set up coal washeries.

The Second Plan called for more detailed geological surveys of existing coal fields and new potential coal producing areas. Because of difficulties in obtaining qualified personnel and equipment, expansion of the Geological Survey of India and the Indian Bureau of Mines did not progress as rapidly as had been hoped during the First Plan.[8]

7. G.o.I., *First Plan*, pp. 165-67.
8. G.o.I., *Second Plan*, pp. 375-80.

Third Five Year Plan

Although the Second Plan goal of producing 60 million tons of coal per year by 1960-61 was not met, production in the last quarter was at an annual rate of about 60 million tons. Hence, capacity existed at the beginning of the Third Plan to produce 60 million tons annually. The aim of the Third Plan was to increase this to an annual rate of 97 million tons by the end of the Plan. Of the 37 million tons in additional production capacity, 20 million tons was to be achieved in the public sector and 17 million tons in the private sector. Because the government policy was to reserve new fields for the public sector, the private sector portion was to be met from the expansion of existing mines and leaseholds. In the public sector, the Third Plan specifically called for the expansion of the Singareni Collieries in Andhra Pradesh and the Neyveli lignite project in Tamil Nadu, but left the remaining production expansion decisions to the National Coal Development Corporation. The Third Plan also called for increased conservation of coking coal by limiting nonessential uses and by increasing capacity in coal washeries to make high grade coal usage more efficient.[9]

Fourth Five Year Plan

Because of the decreased rate of industrial growth brought about by the 1965 war and the agricultural slow-down caused by the 1966-67 drought, the estimated 1973-74 demand for coal was put at 93.5 million tons, which is less than that previously estimated for the end of the Third Plan. During the Fourth Plan, production of coking coal was scheduled to increase from 17 million tons to 23 million tons to meet the capacity requirements of the planned industrial investment. High priority was given to investments expected to achieve this increase in coking coal production. The situation with respect to non-coking coal was less critical. Production capacity of non-coking coal was expected to increase from 65.2 million tons to 68.1 million tons by the end of the Fourth Plan. Therefore, only small investments were needed to achieve that increase in production capacity. Also, during the Fourth Plan, production of lignite from the Neyveli project in Tamil Nadu was planned to increase from 4 million tons to 6 million tons to provide coal for the increased power generation capacity at the Neyveli power station. The total investment in coal production envisaged for the Fourth Plan including both continuing and new schemes amounted to about Rs. 115 crores.[10]

9. G.o.I., *Third Plan*, pp. 133-35.
10. G.o.I., *Fourth Plan*, pp. 321-22, 328.

Summary of first four plans

The growth in coal production over the planning period is shown in Table 21. From 1955-56 to 1974-75 coal production has increased at an average rate of about 4.4 percent annually, although the production increase averaged only 2.6 percent per year over the last six years of that period.

From the beginning of the First Plan through 1970-71, the share of coal produced in the public sector increased, but the absolute amount of coal produced by the private sector also increased. Opening of new coal fields was reserved to the public sector, but some exceptions were allowed in the early years, and expansion of old fields in the private sector was permitted. In the Second Plan the policy of allowing only public sector development was reinforced and strengthened.[11] In 1971-72, almost all privately owned coking coal

Table 21. Coal production in India (million tons).

Year	Public sector	Private sector	Total
1955-56	4.40	34.00	38.40
1956-57	4.85	36.09	40.94
1957-58	5.37	39.44	44.81
1958-59	5.67	41.01	46.68
1959-60	7.15	41.44	48.59
1960-61	10.59	45.08	55.67
1961-62	8.88	46.30	55.18
1962-63	11.66	51.79	63.45
1963-64	12.48	52.65	65.13
1964-65	11.91	50.87	62.78
1965-66	13.64	54.09	67.73
1966-67	13.51	55.05	68.56
1967-68	14.45	54.07	68.52
1968-69	16.52	54.89	71.41
1969-70	17.47	58.24	75.71
1970-71	17.85	55.10	72.95
1971-72	25.27	46.79	72.06
1972-73	41.37	35.50	76.87
1973-74	75.46	2.60	78.06
1974-75	88.41		88.41
1975-76 (through February)	89.46		89.46

Sources: S. Mohan Kumaramangalam *Coal Industry in India*, p. 77 (through 1972-73); and personal communication with Mrs. Anjali Sen, Coal India Limited.

11. G.o.I., *Second Plan*, p. 378.

mines were taken over by the State. In 1973, all remaining non-coking coal mines were nationalized. With the cabinet reorganization of October, 1974, management of the entire coal industry is concentrated in a department of the new Ministry of Energy.[12]

Fifth Five Year Plan

During the Fifth Plan, the output of both coking and non-coking coal is expected to grow substantially from 79 million tons in 1973-74 to 135 million tons in 1978-79. Estimated 1973-74 production of coking coal was 17.0 million tons, and the projection for the end of the Fifth Plan is 32.0 million tons, an annual growth rate of 13.5 percent. For non-coking coal, the estimated 1973-74 production was 62.0 million tons and the Fifth Plan target is 103.0 million tons, an annual growth rate of 10.7 percent.[13]

OIL AND NATURAL GAS

Historically, relatively little petroleum resource development has occurred in India. There was no specific allocation for petroleum exploration or development in India's First Five Year Plan. Three main arguments were used to limit initial government investment in this area:

1. Oil exploration is very risky and developing nations should concentrate their investment spending in more certain projects.
2. Because of the great risk involved, a large effort is necessary in order to assure some success; in other words, a small effort would be unsatisfactory because the individual risk on exploration projects is unacceptably high.
3. The international oil companies have the experience and technical know-how to successfully explore and develop petroleum resources and they are sufficiently diversified.[14]

However, in the Second Plan, the Government of India entered the oil exploration business with some exploration activity and a large personnel training program. In the Third Plan the government significantly increased its exploration and also expanded the petroleum transportation systems. The Third Plan also marked the beginning of Government participation in the market-

12. Henderson, p. 51.
13. G.o.I., *Fifth Plan in Outline*, pp. 24-25.
14. Tanzer, p. 117.

ing of petroleum products. Total expenditures on petroleum increased from Rs. 26 crores in the Second Plan to Rs. 115 crores in the Third Plan.[15] In the Fourth Plan the pace of exploration, production, refining, and marketing was increased significantly with Rs. 187 crores being allocated to exploration, Rs. 85 crores for refineries, and Rs. 30 crores for marketing.[16]

The target for the Fifth Plan is to increase annual petroleum production from 7.7 million tons (estimated for 1973-74) to 12.0 million tons, an annual increase of 9.3 percent. The original plan allocation was Rs. 436 crores for exploration and development and Rs. 500 crores for oil refining and distribution.[17] Since the issuance of the original plan, the budget for exploration and development has been quadrupled to Rs. 16,900 crores. Most of this budget increase is allocated to onshore and offshore exploration and to development of the offshore fields already discovered.[18] India has good prospects for meeting and exceeding the Fifth Plan target for oil production.

NUCLEAR ENERGY

There was no specific allocation in the First Plan to nuclear energy development. The program in scientific and industrial research followed more applied and traditional lines. By the beginning of the Second Plan, India was committed to the development of her atomic energy raw materials and implementation of nuclear energy electric power generating facilities. An atomic reactor at Trombay was scheduled for completion early in the Second Plan. A number of projects were planned for exploration, extraction, or processing of nuclear raw materials. For example, the capacity of the monazite processing plant at Alwaye in Kerala was to be doubled during the Second Plan. Monazite is the raw material containing thorium, uranium and zirconium which is very abundant in Kerala. A number of other projects were planned for processing raw ores into products useful in nuclear power generation.[19]

The Third Plan included a provision for establishing a nuclear power plant and called for expansion of research in atomic energy. Rs. 35 crores was allocated to the Department of Atomic Energy for research, and Rs. 51 crores to constructing the atomic power plant. In addition, scientific research in a large number of related areas was expanded significantly.[20]

15. G.o.I., *Third Plan*, pp. 135-36.
16. G.o.I., *Fourth Plan*, p. 323, 329.
17. G.o.I., *Fifth Plan*, 2: 140, 146-47.
18. Aulbridge, p. 50.
19. G.o.I., *Second plan*, pp. 525-27.
20. G.o.I., *Third Plan*, pp. 165-67 and 108-09.

Investment in nuclear energy continued in the Fourth Plan with a planned total of Rs. 64.3 crores. Most of this amount was allocated to the expansion or continuation of schemes for production or processing of atomic minerals, production of electronic equipment, or research and development.[21] In addition, more funding was provided for basic research in atomic energy under allocations to research institutions like the Council of Scientific and Industrial Research.[22]

During the Fifth Plan, .705 million kilowatts of nuclear generating capacity is scheduled to be completed. In addition, the Atomic Energy Commission is planning to construct a prototype 40 megawatt Fast Breeder Thermal Reactor. This reactor will use plutonium and thorium for fuel and convert the thorium into fissile material in the process.[23]

SUMMARY

Reviewing government activity in the energy sector over the past twenty-five years provides a useful background for the analysis of future energy policy. During the first four plans, progress in electric power development consistently fell behind targets by large amounts. Power supply is a major problem in the energy sector in India today. Coal production lagged somewhat behind targets, but not so badly as did power generation. The major problem in the coal sector is coking coal which is in short supply. Oil and natural gas development proceeded at a very slow pace up until the Fourth Plan. With higher oil prices causing a tremendous drain on foreign exchange earnings, oil exploration and development has stepped up markedly since 1974. With respect to nuclear energy, India clearly has the capability to proceed in this direction, but like many nations, India is choosing not to invest large amounts into this energy resource.

Development of other energy resources such as biogas and solar energy was limited to research and development activity or limited pilot scale applications. This review of energy resource development in the five year plans provides a backdrop for the analysis of specific energy sectors in Chapters 4, 5 and 6.

21. G.o.I., *Fourth Plan*, pp. 323, 325, and 330.
22. Ibid., pp. 380-85.
23. G.o.I., *Fifth Plan*, 2: 122-23.

4. Oil and natural gas

This chapter provides a brief history of the oil industry in India and a discussion of the institutional structure of oil exploration and production in India today. A detailed analysis is provided of the production sharing contracts currently existing between the Oil and Natural Gas Commission and foreign exploration companies. The efficiency of this system of leasing potential petroleum areas is compared with other leasing systems using an analytical model developed for the evaluation of petroleum leasing policy. Using the results of the empirical analysis of the Indian leasing system, suggestions are made for future lease arrangements with foreign exploration companies.

BRIEF HISTORY OF THE OIL INDUSTRY IN INDIA

At the time of independence, the oil industry in India was dominated by foreign corporations, mostly of British origin. Over one half of the petroleum sales in India were accounted for by Burmah-Shell, an equal partnership between the Burmah Oil Company of Scotland and Shell Oil Company of Holland. Other companies were the Standard Vacuum Oil Company, an equal partnership between Standard of New Jersey and Mobil Oil, and Caltex, an equal partnership between Standard of California and Texaco.[1]

During the early five year plans, conflicts began between the private foreign oil companies and the Government of India. These conflicts were intensified in the late 1950s by the foreign exchange pressure caused by oil import costs. By 1960 the Government of India had persuaded the foreign companies to build refineries in India and to import crude oil instead of refined products.[2] But a further cause of conflict was the private companies' refusal to import low priced Soviet crude oil for processing in their Indian refineries. The Soviet Union offered to supply India with crude oil on barter terms at very com-

1. Tanzer, p. 168.
2. Ibid., p. 178.

petitive prices. Western companies refused to refine the Soviet oil and labeled it as 'political oil'. This disagreement increased the tension between the Government of India and the foreign oil companies.

A further source of tension was the prices which were paid for Middle Eastern oil by the foreign companies. The Government of India contended that the prices were too high given the competitive market situation. There were also disagreements about what costs should be included in setting the refined product price in India for the foreign companies. For all of these reasons, the Government of India began to take an increasing role in the oil industry in India. Since the mid 1960s, the Government of India has been operating under a policy of eventually acquiring complete ownership of all oil operations in India.[3]

CURRENT STRUCTURE OF OIL OPERATIONS IN INDIA

At the current time, the Government of India controls 90 to 95 percent of all oil and gas operations in India, and has begun negotiations with Burmah Oil Company for a complete take over of all oil operations in India.[4] In addition, all future oil exploration on land is reserved to the Oil and Natural Gas Commission, the operating unit of the Ministry of Petroleum and Chemicals.

Recently the Oil and Natural Gas Commission has had two important successes in its offshore operations off the northwestern coast of India (near Bombay). The two discoveries are expected to contain recoverable reserves in excess of two billion barrels (275 million tons). These discoveries tripled the proven reserves of India and are the first major finds for the Oil and Natural Gas Commission. The Government of India reportedly considers these discoveries '. . . a vindication of its long standing go-it-alone policy.'[5]

Recently, however, this policy has been modified by leasing offshore areas to non-Indian groups of firms. Of the fifteen offshore areas that have been identified as potentially oil bearing, three have been leased to foreign exploration companies. These leases are in the form of production sharing contracts between the Oil and Natural Gas Commission and private exploration companies.

3. Ibid., pp. 168-222.
4. Auldridge, p. 50.
5. Ibid.

PRODUCTION SHARING CONTRACTS

Production sharing leases are a type of constrained royalty or profit share system whereby the contractor is allowed to recover cost plus a profit allowance with the remainder of the oil going to the lessor (Government of India). The lessee pays all exploration and development expenses which are recovered from his portion of the oil if a discovery is made.

General provisions

Two production sharing contracts have been signed with U.S. firms – the contract for the Bengal-Orissa area is with the Carlsberg-Natomas group and the Kutch Basin contract is with the Reading and Bates Oil and Gas Company group. Although there are minor differences between the two contracts, they both have the same structure. Both are production sharing contracts and each covers about 28,000 sq. km. (6.9 million acres) initially.

At the end of a maximum two year exploration period the contractor must select an area of 5,000 square kilometers (1.2 million acres) for further exploration operations and surrender the remaining area (approximately 23,000 square kilometers) to the Oil and Natural Gas Commission together with all the seismic and geophysical data collected up to that time. At the end of the third year, the area is further reduced to 2,500 square kilometers (.6 million acres) with the remainder being turned back to the Oil and Natural Gas Commission. At the end of the seventh year the contractor is left with producing areas within the 2,500 square kilometer area.

According to the terms of the contract, the companies are required to commit themselves to a work program with a minimum level of expenditure for seismic surveys and exploratory wells in each operating period. The total exploration and development period is limited to eleven years. A joint management committee between the Oil and Natural Gas Commission and the private contractor supervises the operations and approves the annual budget and work program for each company.

Once production begins, up to 40 percent of the oil produced in each year is granted to the lessee to recover the cost of exploration and development subject to the constraint that the recovery of cost must be spread over at least four years. In other words, the initial exploration and development costs incurred by the company are recovered through a portion of the oil, termed cost oil, which may be up to 40 percent of the production in each of the first four years and each additional year that is required to recover the initial cost of exploration and development.

The remainder of the oil is called profit oil and is shared between the Oil and Natural Gas Commission and the private contractor with shares dependent upon the level of production. For the first 18.25 million barrels produced each year, the company's share is 35 percent of the profit oil and the Oil and Natural Gas Commission retains 65 percent of the profit oil. For production levels higher than 18.25 million barrels per year the marginal shares change according to the share structure shown in Table 22. In addition, 17 percent of the contractor's profit share must be delivered to India at no cost to meet the domestic requirements for oil in India.[6] This requirement effectively reduces the contractor's share of profit oil by 17 percent. For production levels up to 18.25 million barrels per year, the contractor's share becomes 29 percent instead of 35 percent as shown in Table 22. Furthermore, all of the remaining cost oil and profit oil must be sold to the Oil and Natural Gas Commission for fair market value so long as India is not self sufficient in petroleum. Fair market value is defined as the international price of oil delivered to India.

Table 22. Share structure for profit oil.

Production range			
barrels/day (in thousands)	barrels/year (in millions)	Marginal share to company	Marginal share to G.o.I.
up to 50	up to 18.25	35.0	65.0
50-75	18.25-27.375	32.5	67.5
75-100	27.375-36.5	30.0	70.0
100-150	36.5-54.75	27.5	72.5
150-250	54.75-91.25	25.0	75.0
250 +	91.25 +	20.0	80.0

Source: Company officials, Reading and Bates Oil Company; Government officials, Government of India.

Once the private contractor has recovered his exploration and development costs through cost oil and twice that amount through profit oil (i.e., once he has recovered three times his initial cost), the contractor's share of oil falls to about one quarter of what it was up to that point. In other words, once cost has been recovered three times, the contractor's share falls to one fourth the levels shown in Table 22. The 17 percent domestic requirement is eliminated

6. This provision, adapted from the Indonesian contracts, is merely a device for increasing the government's share of profit oil. The contracts are written in this manner (instead of directly changing the shares) for political reasons. Receiving a portion of the oil at no cost is viewed as being more attractive politically than simply receiving a greater share of total production.

at this point. For the remainder of the lease, the contractor's share of oil is 5 to 9 percent of the total oil produced.

The contract also provides that the Oil and Natural Gas Commission has the right to participate in up to 10 percent equity of the contract upon the declaration of a commercial discovery of oil. The price of this 10 percent share is determined by the cost incurred up to that point in time. The contract also calls for complete transfer of ownership and management of the lease area to the Oil and Natural Gas Commission by mutual agreement after eleven years from the effective date of the contract. The contractor is required to use Indian personnel and equipment, goods, and services subject to comparable price, quality, and availability. The contract also requires the lessee to pay a small cash bonus upon signing the contract and production bonuses upon commercial discovery.[7]

Natural gas production is to be utilized in the Indian market so long as the supply is needed. Exports are permitted only if the gas cannot be utilized in India.[8]

The Oil and Natural Gas Commission contract (off the Tamil Nadu coast) with the Asamera group of Canada is similar to the one described above but incorporates some differences. The major difference in the Asamera contract is that the Oil and Natural Gas Commission has equity participation from the beginning with an initial share of 35 percent. If a commercial deposit is discovered, the Oil and Natural Gas Commission has the right to increase its share by another 15 percent at cost. The initial lease area and exploration turn-back provisions of the Asamera contract are essentially the same as those described above for the two American firms.

The terms for recovery of cost oil are somewhat different in the Asamera contract. The recovery of cost oil must be spread over a minimum of five years and subject to the constraint that no more than 30 percent of the value of annual production be assigned to the recovery of cost. The share structure for profit oil is also somewhat different in the Asamera contract. At the lowest level of production, 70 percent of the profit oil goes to the Oil and Natural Gas Commission and 30 percent to the contractor with the government share increasing to 85 percent at the highest level of production.

Having the right to 50 percent of equity participation in the Asamera contract, the actual share of produced oil that the Indian government will be

7. For example, the signature bonus on the Reading and Bates contract is $ 1.25 million. There is also a commercial discovery bonus of $ 1 million payable on the first day of production and production bonuses of $ 3 million at the attainment of 40,000 barrels of oil per day and each incremental 40,000 barrels per day.

8. According to company representatives, the contracts were written assuming oil discovery and would have to be renegotiated in the event of a large non-associated natural gas discovery.

entitled to is quite high. At the lowest level of production, India would be entitled to 85 percent of the profit oil (70 percent of its own share and 15 percent of its share of the contractor's oil). Once the costs are recovered twice out of profit oil and the contractor's share falls to one fourth of the original level, the government will be entitled to 96.25 percent of the total oil at the lowest level of production and 97.5 percent of the total oil at the highest level of production. The other features of the Asamera contract are essentially similar to the contracts with the two American firms.

Tax provisions

One important feature of the contracts is that the Oil and Natural Gas Commission pays all of the Indian taxes for the private contractor. The taxes are computed using the grossing up method based on net income. For example, if the net income or profit share of the private contractor were $100,000, and the corporate tax rate in India were 73 percent, taxes would be figured by determining what amount of gross income would yield an after tax net income of $100,000. The calculation is performed by dividing the net income, in this case $100,000, by one minus the average tax rate, in this case .27. This yields a gross income of $373,000 and a tax payment of $273,000 which the Oil and Natural Gas Commission pays to the Government of India for the private contractor. The contractor receives a receipt from the Oil and Natural Gas Commission and the Government of India indicating that the taxes have been assessed and paid for the private contractor by the Oil and Natural Gas Commission. This feature of the contract is very important in terms of private profitability for the American and Canadian companies.

The reason this tax provision is so important is that the private companies are allowed to obtain a credit on their American taxes equal to the total amount of foreign taxes paid. This credit may not exceed their American tax liability on the income received from foreign operations. In this example, the foreign firm would report a gross income of $373,000, and assuming no further deductions would calculate an American tax of 48 percent of that amount or $179,000. But the company has a tax credit from the Indian government of $273,000 so the total American tax bill of $179,000 is credited by the Indian tax payments. The income received from Indian operations is not subject to any American corporate income tax.

It is this feature of the American and Canadian tax law that allows the American companies to take such a small share of the actual production while still maintaining a profitable investment. Recently this tax provision has been contested by the Internal Revenue Service for production sharing contracts.

The implications of changes in this tax provision will be discussed below.[9]

RESOURCE LEASING POLICY EVALUATION MODEL

This section provides a detailed specification and description of the leasing model used in this analysis. The model incorporates a number of factors important for public policy decisions into a framework of private market behavior. Economic and engineering considerations relevant to private producer decision making are included so that the model may be useful for quantitatively testing the effects of a wide range of public policy alternatives.

This model may be used for analyzing a wide variety of leasing systems and strategies. The description provided here is not limited to the Indian leasing system; rather, it is written in a general framework to cover analysis of the Indian system as well as those systems with which it will be compared. The model may also be used for leasing analysis of other resources such as coal, so references to this potential also will appear in the model description.

The model description generally follows the solution algorithm of the computerized model. For each major step in the model calculations, the theoretical background will be presented and the actual model relationships will be described. The model algorithm depends in part on the way in which installed capacity (Q_0) is input into the model. Figure 2 is a flow diagram for the simulation when Q_0 is given exogenously. In Figure 3, Q_0 is determined endogenously by the model. The model description will follow these two flow diagrams and will separately describe the solution algorithm with exogenous Q_0 and with Q_0 determined endogenously. It may be helpful for the reader to refer back and forth between these figures and the text. To make the description easier to follow, a list of all input variables specifically used in this text with the computer code, the symbol used in this description, and a brief definition is provided in Table 23. All symbols in the text and future references to variable names will refer to the variable definitions in Table 23.

After the variables are read in and stored if necessary, the first step in the model solution is to run completely through the model once using mean values for all input variables. This step determines the after tax net present value (ATNPV) if all mean values are used and converts that value into a

9. The entire discussion on production sharing contracts was based on interviews with Government of India officials in Delhi (December 1975) and conversations with officials of Natomas Oil Company (May 1975) and Reading and Bates Oil Company (May-June 1976). In addition, copies of major contract provisions were supplied by the Government of India and Reading and Bates Oil Company. The author is very grateful to all these parties for their cooperation in this research.

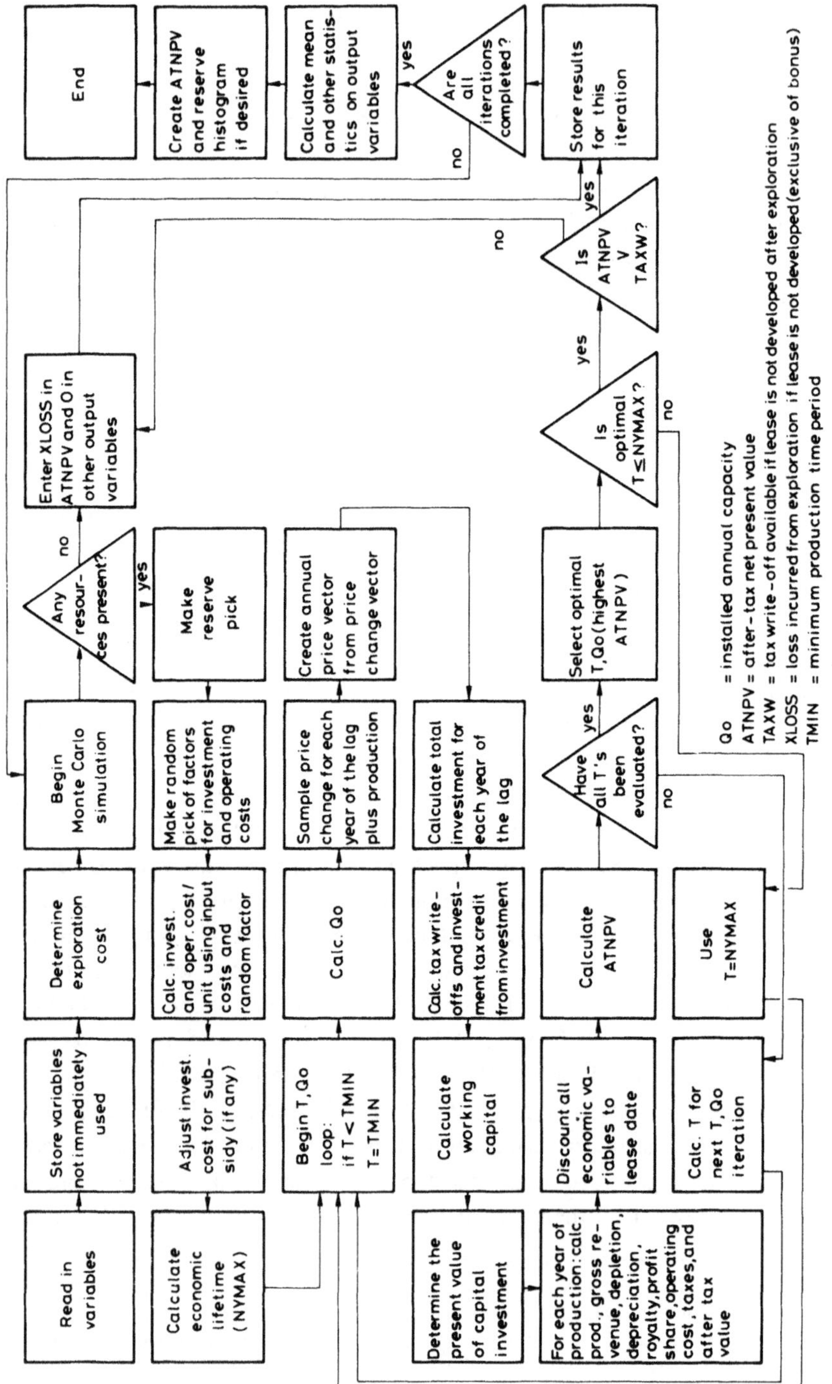

Figure 2. Flow diagram for simulation model with endogenous Q_o.

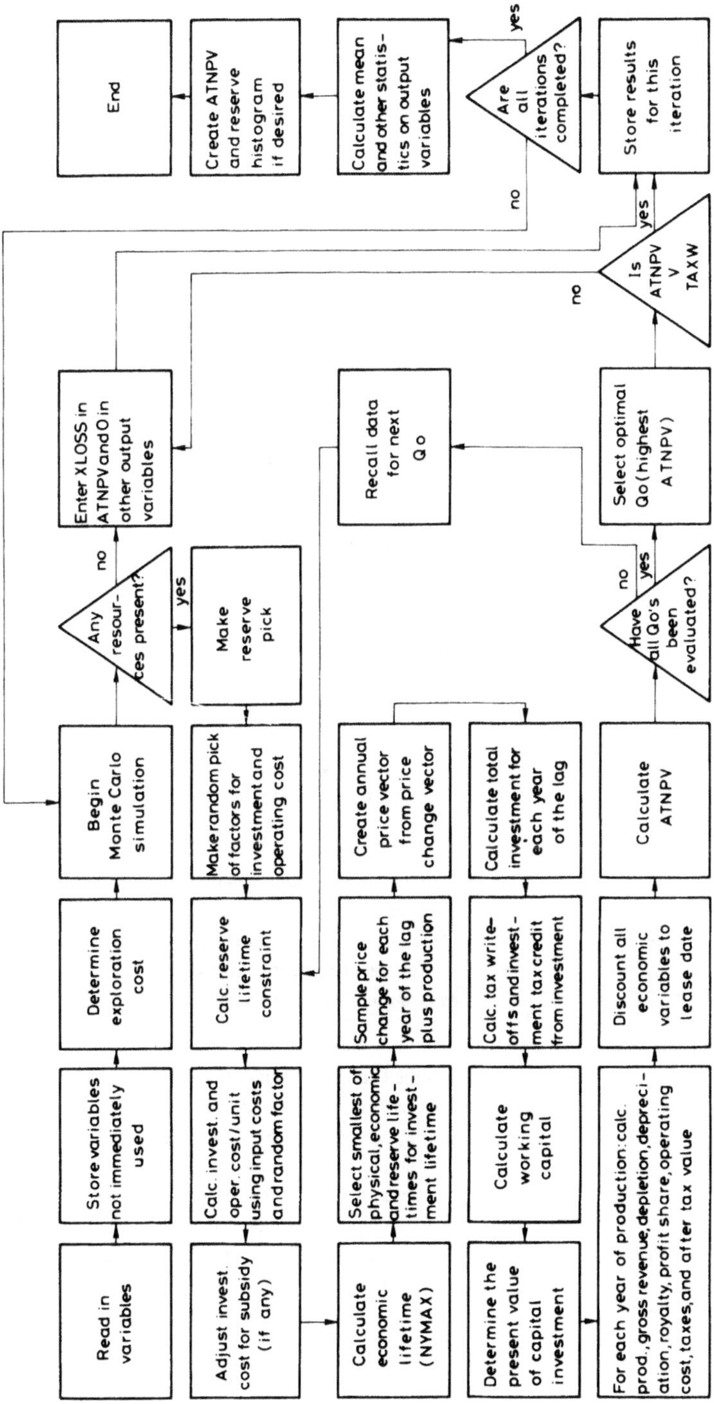

Qo = installed annual capacity
ATNPV = after-tax net present value
TAXW = tax write-off available if lease is not developed after exploration
XLOSS = loss incurred from exploration if lease is not developed (exclusive of bonus)

Figure 3. Flow diagram for simulation model with input Q_o.

Table 23. Input variables for the generalized resource policy model.

Symbol	Computer code	Definition
Price related:		
P_0	PPØ	Initial price for the primary resource
GP_0	SPØ	Initial price for the secondary resource
P_1	P1M	Mean of the normal distribution for annual price change (primary resource)
GP_1	S1M	Mean of the normal distribution for annual price change (secondary resource)
Geologic:		
DTRSK	DTRSK	Chance that the lease contains no recoverable resources
R	RMEAN	Mean of reserve distribution
β	BETA	Geologic parameter
AGFAC	AGFAC	Factor for calculating the amount of associated gas or other resource
F	IFLATP	Length of the initial flat production period (years)
a	A	Production decline rate (%)
Economic and tax related:		
λ	RØYRT	Royalty rate (%)
s	STR	Severance tax rate (%)
α	ALPHA	Investment salvageable (%)
Ω	ØMEGA	Investment tax credit rate (%)
z	Z	Depletion rate (revenue) (%)
$\emptyset$	PHI	Federal tax rate (%)
N	N	Depreciation period (years)
r	R	Discount rate (%)
B_o	BCØN	Constant used to calculate BØNUS
B_1	BFAC	Factor used to calculate BØNUS
T_p	LT	Maximum physical lifetime (years)
Production and cost related:		
Q_o	Q	Installed capacity (annual)
c	C	Cost per unit of installed capacity
k_o	K	Operating cost per unit
θ	THETA	Annual change in operating cost (%)
L	LAG	Length of the development period (years)
f	F	Proportion of investment expended in each year
Y	YZ	Proportion of yearly investment which is tangible
RENT	RENT	Annual rent per acre
h_i	BPP	Factor used to determine production during build up period (IBP)

bonus payment to be used in subsequent calculations. This conversion is assumed to be linear according to equation (4):

$$(4) \qquad \text{BONUS} = B_0 + B_1 \cdot \text{ATNPV}$$

where B_0 and B_1 are the input values BCON and BFAC, respectively.[10] Optionally, the bonus may also be recalculated after any number of Monte Carlo iterations for use in subsequent iterations.

The exploration phase of resource development

The next step in the model solution is to determine the exploration cost for the lease tract or area in question. For example, oil exploration costs are a function of the number of wells to be drilled per acre, the number of acres in the tract, and the cost per well as illustrated in equation (5):

$$(5) \qquad EC = \text{Wells/acre} \times \text{acres} \times \text{dollars/well}$$

Tax write-offs from expensed investment and rent payments are subtracted from the tax vector. Exploration expenses each year minus the tax savings are entered into the after tax value vector.

In addition to calculating the total net expenses of exploration, the potential tax write-off available to the company if the lease is not developed is also calculated at this time. This potential tax write-off is the bonus payment and the remaining depreciable base of exploration expenses multiplied by the tax rate. This potential tax write-off is compared later in the program with the potential present value of the lease if developed to decide whether or not it is advantageous to develop the lease.

Uncertainty and the Monte Carlo analysis

Once exploration cost is determined, the Monte Carlo simulation begins. A number of the variables used in this model are considered uncertain and are subject to Monte Carlo simulation analysis. Any or all of the following variables may be selected randomly in the Monte Carlo simulation: annual change in price, contingency factor for investment cost, contingency factor for operating cost, the chance that the lease area contains no resources, and the amount of resources actually present. For policy analysis, it is important

10. If B_0 and B_1 are set equal to 0 and 1, respectively, the bonus will equal ATNPV. For the Indian system, B_0 and B_1 are equal to zero because the signature bonus is negligible.

to determine the potential effects on private decisions of uncertainty with respect to future prices, production costs, and reserves. Using the mean (average) values of probability distributions is inadequate for this analysis because only outputs resulting from these mean values are produced. No measure of the spread (variance) of potential outcomes is obtained. In other words, in the absence of some type of simulation, no measure of the potential riskiness of the final outcome is derived. For policy purposes, it is desirable to learn not only how the mean output values are affected by various policy options but also how the variance or range of the outcomes is changed.

For example, suppose two policy options have identical effects on the means of relevant policy objectives (model outputs), have identical costs (in whatever terms cost is measured), but have differential effects on the expected outcome variances. Naturally, the policy maker would want to consider the difference in variance in his policy decision. Also, because of non-linear transformations in the model operations, the simulation results may differ from the analysis using mean input values. Trade-offs between changes in means, differences in relative cost, and variances must be weighed by the decision makers.

Monte Carlo simulation is one technique for handling the problem of uncertainty in input values and estimating the variance in potential outcomes. Rather than using point estimates of uncertain input variables, an assumed probability distribution is provided from which samples are taken to be used as inputs for the analysis. The process of sampling each variable from its unique probability distribution and performing the model calculations is repeated many times to produce a range of model output values. A frequency distribution of these output values can be derived and the mean and variance of the expected outcomes determined. In performing this type of simulation we replace the unknown actual population of future prices, costs and reserves by an assumed probability distribution from which samples are drawn. By sampling many times it is possible to generate many possible combinations of prices, costs, and reserves that together produce outcomes, each in the appropriate proportion.[11]

Any type of probability distribution may theoretically be specified for the uncertain variables. Figures 4, 5, 6, and 7 depict the normal, triangular, uniform and lognormal distributions, respectively. The uncertain variables used in this model and the type of distribution which is used for each variable are listed in Table 24.

11. W. R. King, *Probability for Management Decisions* (New York: John Wiley and Sons, Inc., 1968), p. 303.

Table 24. Distributions used for uncertain variables.

Variable	Distribution
Annual price change	Normal or truncated normal
Investment cost contingency factor	Triangular
Operating cost contingency factor	Triangular
Presence or absence of resources (Bernouli)	Uniform
Amount of reserves	Lognormal or normal

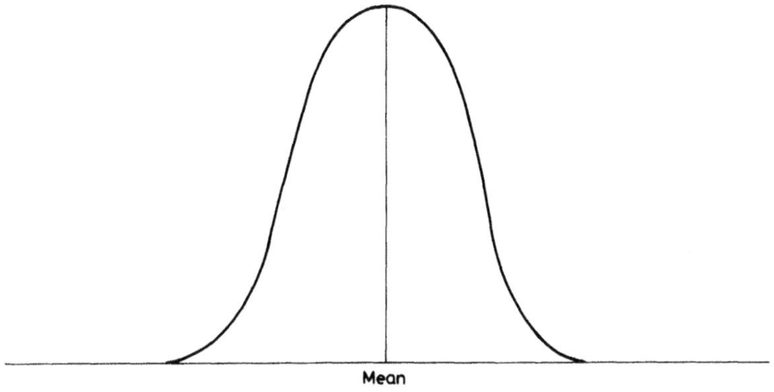

Figure 4. Normal distribution used for annual price change and reserves.

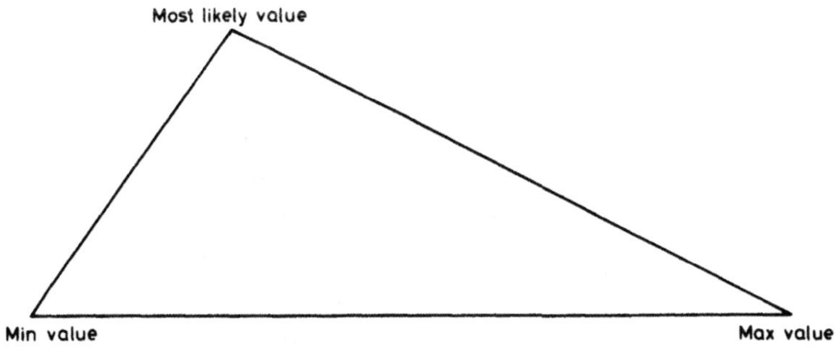

Figure 5. Triangular distribution.

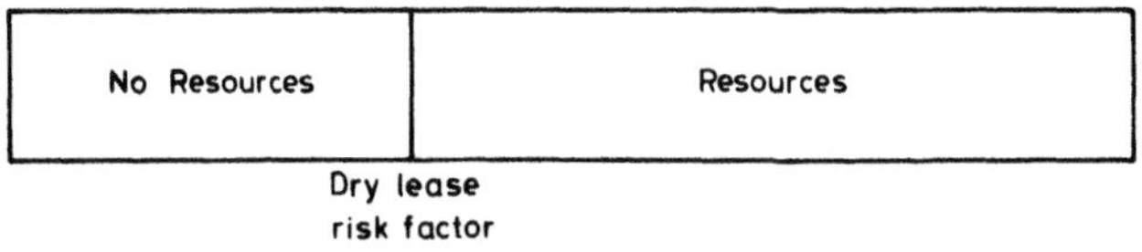

Figure 6. Uniform distribution.

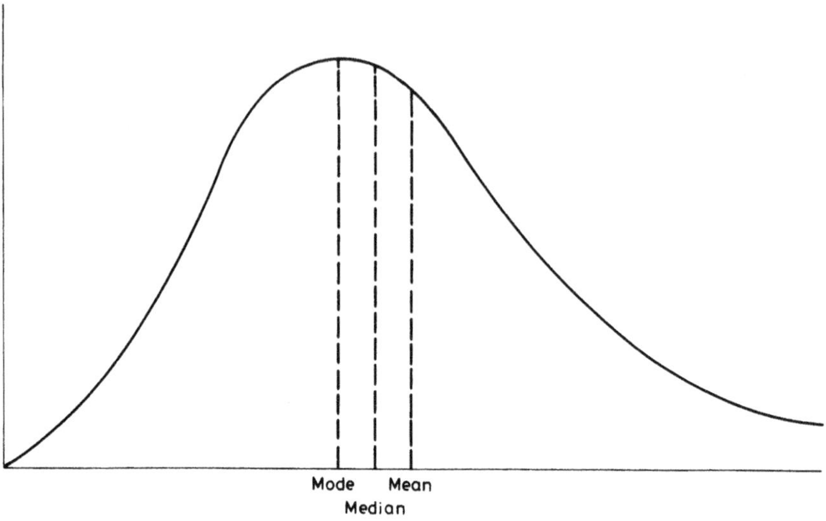

Figure 7. Lognormal distribution.

Future resource prices

Uncertainty in future resource prices is handled by randomly selecting the annual change in price each year from a normal distribution with a specified mean and variance. This vector of sample annual price changes together with the initial resource price, P_0, is used to create a vector of initial prices for each year of potential lease duration. Equation (6) illustrates this process:

$$(6) \qquad P_0(t+1) = P_0(t) \cdot e^{P_1(t)}$$

$P_0(t)$ is the initial resource price in year t, $P_1(t)$ is the rate of change in price during year t (from the vector of price change samples), and $P_0(t+1)$ is the initial resource price in year $(t+1)$. This vector of initial prices for each year and the vector of price changes during each year are used in the model computations to determine gross revenue for each year of production. Since this procedure is repeated independently for each Monte Carlo iteration, a separate price distribution emerges for each year of the production period. Because the annual price change has a compound effect upon the initial price, the mean and variance of these annual price distributions would also change through time.

It is important to understand that the price change used in this analysis is the expected price change in excess of general inflation. It is not the total expected change in price of the resource; rather, it is the difference between the expected change in price of the resource and the expected general rate of inflation in the economy. This same principle applies to investment and operating cost factors. Thus, the relative inflation rate between revenues expected from the resource and cost to obtain the resource is a derivative of the inputs to the model. Because both cost and revenue inflation factors are keyed to general inflation, relative inflation between costs and revenues for a particular investment is automatically accounted for using this procedure.

Investment cost contingency factor

Investment costs are uncertain for at least three reasons, and a cost contingency factor is used to handle this uncertainty. The contingency factor is a percentage of the estimated investment cost and is selected from a triangular distribution with an input minimum, maximum, and most likely value.

One of the most important reasons for a contingency factor in investment cost is that inflation in construction costs in recent years has taken place at a rate higher than the rate of general inflation. Although this experience will not necessarily continue, it is uncertain what the rate will be over the next decade. Since the construction and start-up period may be five years or more, the rate of inflation can have a significant effect on total construction costs. Second, investment costs may be uncertain because technology for extracting and refining some resources is relatively new. For example, sub-sea completions required in some offshore areas represent a new technology. Unforeseen engineering and technical problems could raise investment costs substantially. A third reason for an investment cost contingency factor is that if facilities of the type and scale required have not previously been constructed, the length of the development and construction period cannot be known with certainty. Changes in the assumed period will have a significant impact on the present value of investment costs.

As is evident from the discussion of these factors, the distribution of investment cost uncertainty tends to be one sided. In other words, the risk is mainly on the high side, so the distribution would be expected to be skewed in that direction.

Operating cost contingency factor

The two factors affecting annual operating costs in the model are θ, the annual increase in cost per unit, and K_0, the initial operating cost per unit. For purposes of analysis, θ was assumed to be known and constant throughout the production period, and a triangular distribution of K_0 values was utilized. Uncertainty in initial operating cost arises from the same sources as investment cost (future relative inflation and unforeseen technological difficulties) plus uncertainty in the future cost of environmental protection. Since future government regulations are unknown or are subject to modification, it is difficult to forecast the environmental control costs which must be borne by the private sector. However, once production has begun with technological problems solved and environmental control equipment in place, future changes in operating cost should be subject to less uncertainty. Therefore, the initial operating cost, K_o, was assumed to be uncertain with risk mainly on the high side.

In addition to the factors K_o and θ, *unit* operating costs are also affected by the rate of decline in production. Since total operating costs are determined by the factors described above, unit operating costs rise as production falls. This point is discussed further at a later point in the text.

Presence or absence of resources

This variable is particularly relevant for oil and natural gas production. When some quantity of resource is known with certainty to be present, the variable may be set to zero, and the model then assumes resources are always present on the lease area. When the variable is operative, the random number generator is used to generate a random number between zero and one from a uniform distribution. This random number is then compared with the dry lease risk factor to determine if resources are present. If the random number is greater than or equal to the dry lease risk factor, then resources are assumed to be present and the model computations continue. For example, if the random number generated were .13 and the dry lease risk factor .10, then resources would be present for this iteration. Clearly, if the dry lease risk factor is set at zero, all random numbers between zero and one will be greater than or equal to the dry lease risk factor and resources will always be present.

Amount of reserves

For some resources such as oil and natural gas, the greatest source of uncertainty is the amount of reserves present. For almost all resources some degree of uncertainty about the total quantity of resources in place exists.

Relating to petroleum exploration, a number of researchers have found that the lognormal distribution provides a good fit for experimental data on the size of petroleum deposits.[12] Therefore, the lognormal distribution is used

12. R. S. Uhler and P. G. Bradley, 'A Stochastic Model for Determining the Economic Prospects of Petroleum Exploration Over Large Regions,' *Journal of the American Statistical Association* 65 (June 1970); U.S. Geological Survey. *Geological Estimates of Undiscovered Recoverable Oil and Gas Resources in the United States*, Geological Survey Circular 725, 1975; Kalter, Tyner, and Hughes, pp. 7-13.

for the size distribution of petroleum resources and in other situations where deemed appropriate.

For resources which are not distributed lognormally, the normal distribution may also be used in the simulation program. In either case, the mean and standard deviation and distribution selection are the model inputs.

Model description with Monte Carlo simulation

Once the Monte Carlo simulation begins, each of the procedures is repeated for each iteration of the simulation. In other words, if 200 Monte Carlo iterations are specified, all of the steps from this point on are repeated 200 times. The results of each iteration are stored and used to calculate the mean and other statistics on output variables.

The first step in the Monte Carlo simulation is to determine if there are any resources present on the lease. As described above, the chance of the lease having no resources is an input variable, DTRSK. If no resources are present, the loss incurred from exploration is entered into the after tax net present value vector (ATNPV) and used in calculating the expected present value of the lease over all iterations. The iteration is terminated and a new iteration is begun.

If resources are found on the tract, the next step in the process is to make a random selection of factors to be used in determining total investment and operating costs. A choice of three methods is allowed in making this selection of factors. First, the input investment and operating cost input values may be used without any random component added. In this case, the random selection is bypassed. Alternatively, a cost adjustment factor may be selected from the triangular cost distributions supplied for both investment and operating costs. For both investment and operating cost the minimum adjustment factor, the most likely adjustment factor and the maximum adjustment factor are inputs determining the shape of the triangular density function. For example, the cost factor could range from 0 to .2 with a most likely value of 1. In this case an equilateral triangular density function would be employed. Either the mean of the triangular distribution (the sum of the three vertices divided by three) or a random selection from that distribution may be used to determine the actual cost adjustment factor. The cost adjustment factor is then multiplied by the base cost, and the result added to the base cost. In essence, the random cost component which results from the cost adjustment factor is a sort of contingency. The actual amount of the contingency may be zero (if the base value is used), equal to the mean of the triangular distribution, or randomly selected from the distribution. Normally, the random selection method is used because contingency is considered a random component of total cost. Hence, the random selection method is considered better to reflect actual operating conditions.

The next two steps in the model simulation vary depending upon whether installed capacity is input or determined within the model. If installed capacity is internally determined, the random factors for investment and operating costs are immediately used to determine the investment and operating cost values that will be used for each installed capacity. If installed capacity is an input, associated investment and operating cost values are also inputs unique to each installed capacity. The same random factor is applied to each of the investment and operating cost values for each installed capacity to determine a unique investment and operating cost. There is a fundamental difference between the two versions of the model in that economies of scale with respect to installed capacity are permitted if installed capacity is input to the model, but are not permitted if installed capacity is solved within the model. However, economies of scale with respect to reserve size are permitted under both approaches. Once investment and operating costs are calculated, an investment subsidy may be subtracted if one is used for purposes of policy analysis.

If installed capacity is an input to the model, that capacity together with reserves and other input variables is used to determine the maximum production time horizon which can be used given the installed capacity and the amount of reserves. On the other hand, if installed capacity is solved within the model, a time horizon is determined internally and the corresponding (maximum) installed capacity is solved for within the model. Since each of these procedures represents a different solution to the same basic structural relationship, we will develop that relationship carefully and explain the correlation between the two procedures.

Economic, engineering and geologic relationships

We begin with the relationship between reserves and production. Reserve estimates enter the calculus of profitability both as a basis for the investment and as a constraint on the production from an investment. The production constraint is represented in equation (7):

$$xR \geq \sum_{t=1}^{T} qq(t) \tag{7}$$

where R represents the amount of the resources in place, x the recoverable fraction with a given technology, $qq(t)$ the amount of annual production, and T, the production time horizon. This equation merely states that the sum of production through time can be no greater than the recoverable portion of the reserve in place (with a given technology). Given this constraint, the producer attempts to select an initial plant capacity which will maximize his return through time. In other words, the producer attempts to select the investment which maximizes his after tax net present value of revenue subject to the production constraint.

Assume for the moment that production declines exponentially through time.[13] Annual production may then be expressed as a function of initial installed capacity as in equation (8):

$$qq(t)_i = \int_{t-1}^{t} q(o)_i e^{-at} dt \tag{8}$$

where $q(o)_i$ represents initial installed capacity of the ith plant which is one of a group of possible initial capacities. While this simple relationship between installed capacity and annual production may be adequate for oil resources after a period of time, it is not adequate for other resources or for oil resources during the early production phase. A typical resource production pattern includes a production build-up period during which production is increasing each year as installed capacity is coming on stream followed by a flat production period which continues indefinitely or is followed by a declining production period as shown in Figure 8. Under this scenario, total production during the lease life is given by equation (9):

$$\text{PROD} = q(o)_i \cdot \sum_{j=1}^{B} h_j + q(o)_i \cdot (F\text{-}B) + \int_{0}^{T\text{-}F} q(o)_i e^{-at} dt \tag{9}$$

13. In this text, the variable t is used in two ways. When discrete values or summation is implied as in equation (7), t represents a *time period*; i.e., one year. When t is used in an integral form, it represents a point in (continuous) time as in the right side of equation (8). Equation (8) should be interpreted as the amount of production in year t (left side) is equal to the integral of production from the beginning of the year (point t-1) to the end of the year (point t). The discrete time period values are indexed to begin with *period 1*, and the continuous time value begins at *point 0*. This somewhat unconventional notation was selected to simplify exposition of the model equations which involve both discrete and continuous summation and discounting.

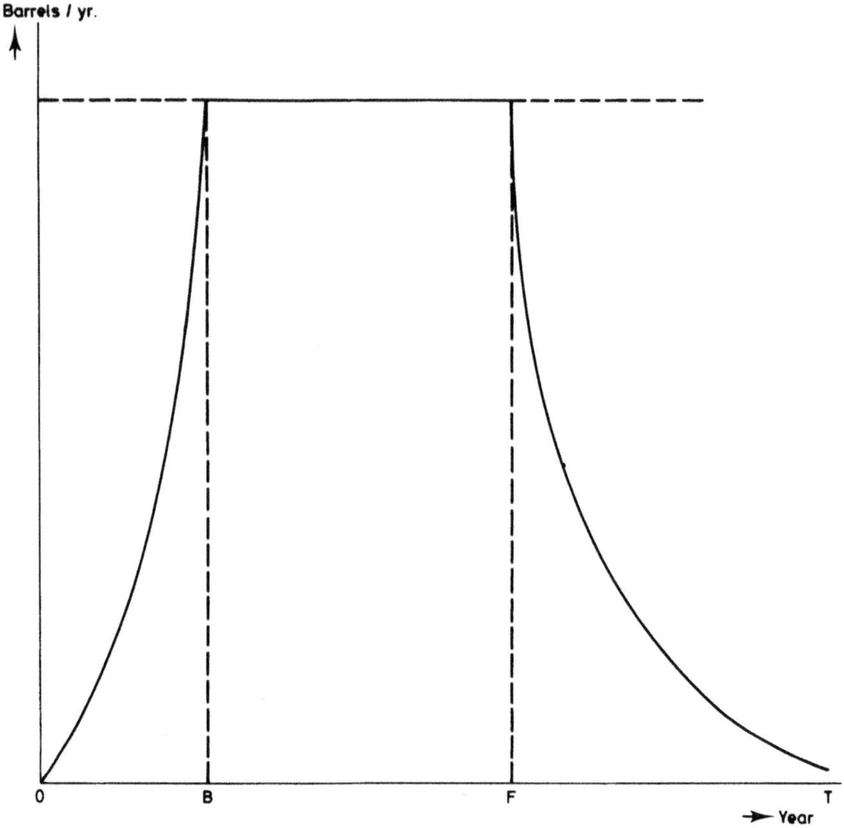

Figure 8. Production profile through time.

where the build-up period is the period between year one and year B, the flat production period is between year B and year F, and the declining production period (perhaps at a zero rate) is the period from F to T, T being the production life of the lease as determined below.[14] Equation (9) gives the sum of production during each of the three phases of production. Production during the build-up period is equal to the sum over the build-up period of the annual factors h_i times installed capacity; production during the flat period is simply the number of years in which production is constant times installed capacity; and production during the decline period is equal to the integral over the number of years production is declining. Recalling from equation (7) that total production must be less than or equal to recoverable reserves we may

14. The integral for the decline period goes from zero to T-F rather than F to T because this integral properly measures the sum of production over the decline period.

now combine equations (7) and (9) to yield the relationship between recoverable resources and installed capacity as in equation (10):[15]

$$(10) \qquad xR - \beta q_o e^{-a} \geq q_o \cdot \sum_{j=1}^{B} h_j + q_o \cdot (F\text{-}B) + \int_{0}^{T\text{-}F} q_o e^{at} dt$$

The β parameter is a geologic variable applicable to oil which relates total recovery to the rate of recovery. (The faster the oil is produced, the lower is total recovery.) If β is equal zero, recoverable reserves, xR, is greater than or equal to production as defined in equation (9).

By assuming that recoverable reserves are exhausted, we may change equation (10) from an inequality to an equality and solve for either q_o or T. Equation (11) represents the solution for equation (10) for T which is used in the case of input q_o:

$$(11) \qquad T = \ln \; [1 + a(-xR/q_o + \beta e^{-a} + \sum h_i + F - B)] \; /{-a} + F$$

Equation (12) represents the solution to equation (10) when installed capacity, q_o, is solved within the model:

$$(12) \qquad q_o = \frac{axR}{[l + a(\beta e^{-a} + \sum h_i + F\text{-}B)\text{-}e^{-a(T-F)}]}$$

Given that q_o and T have been determined either by input or within the model, the production time horizon, T, must be subjected to two constraints before it can be employed. These constraints are the physical and economic lifetimes of the proposed investment. The production time horizon for a given investment can be no greater than the actual physical lifetime of the initial plant. Nor can the production time horizon exceed the time at which variable unit cost of producing the product exceeds the revenues per unit obtained from marketing it. In other words, when the steadily increasing unit costs of production (assuming a rising marginal cost curve) exceed the revenues per unit of production, production would cease.

The first constraint is simply expressed as an exogenously determined con-

15. The notation, $q(o)_i$, is here changed to q_o representing one potential investment, but the reader should be aware that the optimization process covers all available investment opportunities.

stant $T \leq T_p$, where T_p equals the maximum physical lifetime of the investment. The second constraint is the limit obtained when marginal cost equals marginal revenue. Equation (13) states that the economic limit occurs when operating costs plus taxes exceed or equal revenue minus royalties and severance taxes:[16]

$$(13)\quad (1-\lambda-s)P_0e^{P_1(t+L)} \leqq K_0e^{[(\theta+a)t-aF]} + \Phi\left[(1-\lambda-s)P_0e^{P_1(t+L)} - z(1-\lambda-s)P_0e^{P_1(t+L)} - K_0e^{[(\theta+a)t-aF]}\right]$$

Solving equation (13) for the time constraint yields:

$$(14)\qquad T \leqq \left[(ln[\frac{(1\text{-}\Phi)K_0}{(1\text{-}\Phi+\Phi z)(1\text{-}\lambda\text{-}s)P_0}]) - aF - P_l l\right] (P_1 - \theta - a)$$

Note that this equation may be negative or undefined when the rate of change in price is greater than or equal to the decline rate plus the rate of change in unit operating cost ($P1 \geq \theta + a$). The negative sign occurs because the marginal revenue-marginal cost curve intersection is in the negative quadrant to the left of the origin as shown in Figure 9. The correct interpretation for this negative sign is that the economic time constraint is infinite.

We now have each of the equations and relationships necessary to determine the production time horizon. The production time horizon is that T determined in the model either by equation (11) or through the q_0–T optimization procedure, subject to the maximum physical lifetime and the economic lifetime constraint given by equation (14). Hence, the production time horizon is the minimum of the resource exhaustion time period, maximum physical life of the plant, or the economic production time constraint. Mechanically, these equations are determined slightly differently depending

16. Since total operating costs increase by the value θ through time, but remain constant in any time period regardless of the decline rate, unit costs increase at an exponential rate through time. This phenomena is due to equipment obsolescence and/or increased maintenance costs. In notational form, total operating costs in any time, t, are expressed as:

$$q_0K_0e^{\theta t}$$

Thus, unit costs become:

$$q_0K_0e^{\theta t}/q_0e^{-a(t-F)} = K_0e^{[(\theta+a)\,t-aF]}$$

The denominator of this equation is derived from the last term of equation (10).

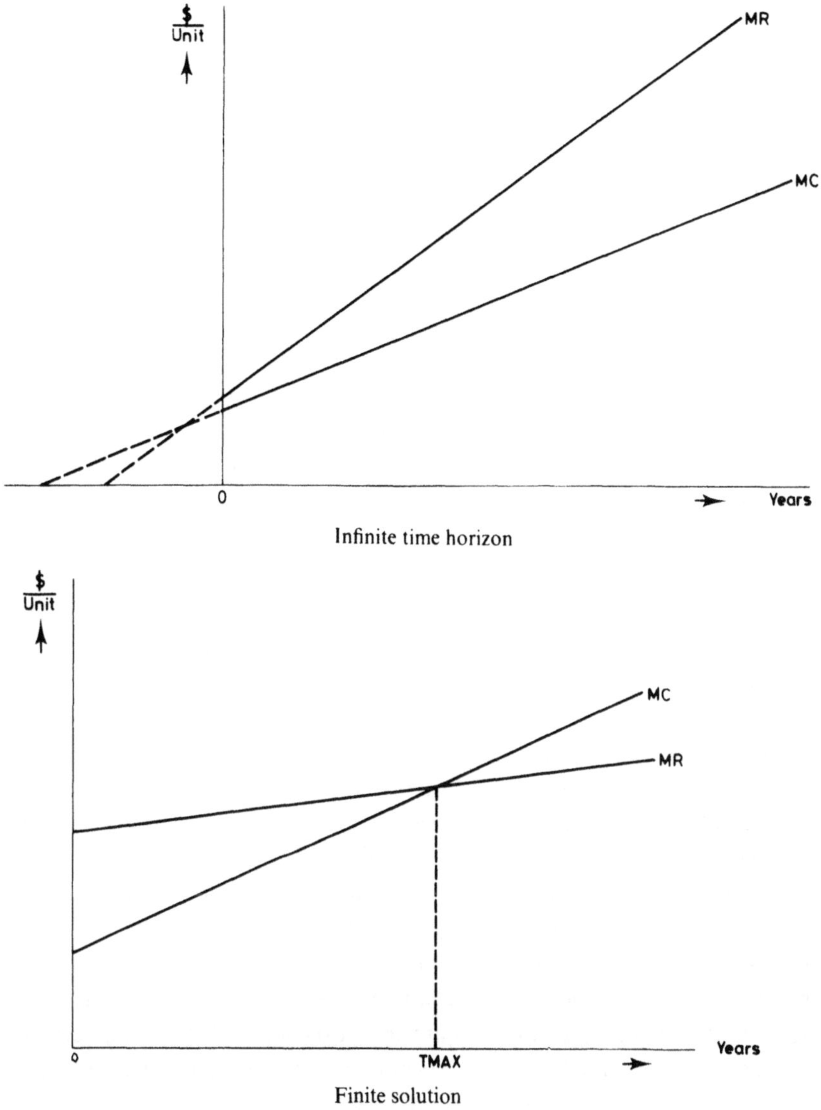

Figure 9. Solution to the economic time horizon.

on whether installed capacity is input or determined by the model as explained above and as outlined in Figures 2 and 3.

For the first q_0–T set to be evaluated in each Monte Carlo iteration, the next step is to create a vector of prices covering each year in the production period. The first step in this process is to create a vector of annual price change covering at least the period from the time of the lease sale to the end of production. This vector may be created by randomly sampling from a normal distribution of price change with an input mean and standard deviation as explained above. Alternatively the mean annual price change may be used for each year in the vector.

If desired, more than one price change distribution may be used in generating the price change vector. The model allows for as many as four unique price change distributions to be input for up to four specified time periods. For example, price could be expected to rise at an annual rate of 8 percent for three years, fall at a rate of 3 percent for six years, remain relatively constant for eight years, and then rise at a rate of 4 percent through the end of production. Each of the expected price change values would have a unique variance, so that the variance as well as the expected value of annual price change can vary through time. The price change vector is created by utilizing the distribution appropriate for each year in the vector.

The next step is to create a vector of prices from the lease time until the end of production using the initial input price P_0 along with the vector of price changes. The vector is created by multiplying the price at the beginning of each year by the exponential price change during that year to get the price at the beginning of the next year. This process is repeated until prices have been generated for each year from the point of the lease sale until the end of production.

The next step is to calculate the investment for each year of the construction and development lag and the discounted value of total capital investment. Total capital investment is determined by multiplying installed capacity, q_0, by the investment cost per unit of installed capacity, C, as determined in the cost subroutine for each resource. To determine the discounted value of total investment, the total investment figure must be multiplied by the percentage of total investment occuring in each year of the development period, and the investment value for each year discounted back to the beginning of the lease. Both development costs and exploration costs for each year are summed together and discounted back to the beginning of the lease. In functional form this relationship is expressed in equation (15):

$$(15) \qquad \mathrm{PVI} = \sum_{j=1}^{L} (q_0 \cdot b \cdot f_i + EX_i) / (1 + R)^i$$

where PVI represents the present value of investment, f_i the factor used to determine the proportion of investment in each year of the lag (L), and EX_i the exploration expense during each year of the lag. The values for total annual investment are then used to calculate depreciation streams for the production period and to calculate expensed investment and investment tax credit.

The model allows any of the following forms of depreciation to be used:

1. No depreciation.
2. Sum of years' digits (SYD) depreciation with input depreciation lifetime (N).
3. Double declining balance (DDB) with automatic conversion to straight line (SL) at the appropriate time – using input depreciation lifetime.
4. Straight line using input depreciation lifetime.
5. Asset depreciation at the same rate as the resource is depleted (annual production/total production) – using the production horizon as depreciation lifetime.
6. SYD with the production horizon as depreciation lifetime.
7. SL with the production horizon as depreciation lifetime.
8. DDB with the production horizon as depreciation lifetime.

According to IRS regulation, capital investment cannot be depreciated until it is placed in service. Therefore, all tangible investment during the development period is depreciated beginning with the first year of production.

Tax savings during the exploration and development periods result from expensed (intangible) investment (EXXINV and EXINV), rental payments during exploration (RENT), and the investment tax credit (IVTC) (at the beginning of production). Tax savings during development are entered as negative values in the tax vector (and consequently as positive values in the after tax value vector).

Working capital is then calculated as a function of the first year's operating cost. Once this calculation is complete, calculations for the production period begin. Annual and total production, gross revenue, operating cost, royalty, severance tax, depletion, profit share or production share, and taxes are calculated. Because many of the equations are in integral form, yet many of the values are needed on an annual basis, integral solutions are obtained over each year of production and then summed over the production period. For example, production is obtained from point zero to the end of year one and then from the beginning of year one to the end of year two and so on through the beginning of the last year of production to the end of the last year of production. These values are then summed to determine total production. In this way both annual and total values can be obtained for variables such as production, profit share, and royalty. A form of continuous discounting is utilized for variables such as gross revenue and operating cost.

The methods used to determine annual production in each year of the production period are described in detail above. In addition to calculating production for the basic resource, production is also calculated for any associated resource such as associated gas with petroleum production. The ratio of production between the major resource and the secondary resource is assumed to be a constant factor. In other words, to determine the production of associated natural gas in each period, the production of oil is multiplied by the factor (AGFAC) to determine the production of natural gas. In the equations that follow the annual production of the major resource will be denoted by q_t and production of the secondary resource will be denoted by g_t.[17]

A number of equations are used in calculating the economic variables for each year of the production period. So that this process may be clearly understood, the equation for gross revenue is presented below in two forms:

1. The integral form divided into annual periods.
2. The computational form actually used in the model.

For simplicity of exposition, the values of F and B are assumed equal to zero. Hence, equations (16) and (17) represent the two forms of the gross revenue equation during the period of production decline:[18]

$$(16) \qquad \mathrm{GR} = q_t P_t \int_0^1 e^{P_1 t} dt + g_t GP_t \int_0^1 e^{GP_1 t} dt$$

$$(17) \qquad \mathrm{GR} = q_t P_t \left(\frac{e^{P_1} - 1}{P_1} \right) + g_t GP_t \left(\frac{e^{GP_1} - 1}{GP_1} \right)$$

Calculation of annual operating cost (OC) proceeds in the same manner as shown in equation (18):

$$(18) \qquad \mathrm{OC} = \left[q_0 K_0 \int_{t-1}^{-t} e^{\theta t} dt \right. = q_0 K_0 \left[\frac{e^{\theta t} - e^{\theta (t-1)}}{\theta} \right]$$

17. In the Indian situation, at least initially, associated gas would most likely be reinjected for pressure maintenance or flared.

18. Actually P_1 and GP_1 are also time indexed variables as explained above, but they are written here in unindexed form for clarity of exposition. P_t and GP_t represent prices at the beginning of year t, and q_t and g_t represent production during year t.

As is clear from equation (18), operating cost throughout the life of an investment is assumed to be dependent upon the initial installed capacity. The marginal cost of extracting the secondary resource is assumed to be zero, *or* included in the cost of extracting the primary resource.

The model contains three annual revenue calculations in addition to the gross revenue calculation in equation (17). The first net revenue (NTREV1) is calculated by subtracting royalty, operating cost, depreciation, severance tax, and rent from gross revenue. In the next step the depletion allowance is calculated. Currently, in the United States only cost depletion is allowed for oil, but for other resources, revenue depletion, cost depletion, or the maximum of the two may be selected. Cost depletion is allowed on the bonus payment and other lease acquisition costs in proportion to the depletion of reserves. To calculate the annual profit share base (NTREV2) depletion is subtracted from NTREV1. Taxable income for each year (NTREV3) is the profit share base minus profit share payments.

After tax income in each year is simply taxable income minus state and federal taxes. After tax value (and other variables) in each year is discounted using the continuous discounting factor shown in equation (19):

$$\text{(19)} \qquad \text{DSC} = \left[\int_{t-1}^{t} e^{-rd} dt \right] = \left[\frac{e^{-rd} - e^{-r(d-1)}}{-r} \right]$$

where d is the production year t plus the development period (lag).

After tax net present value (ATNPV) is calculated by subtracting the present value of investment and lease acquisition cost from the discounted stream of annula after tax values and adding the discounted value of salvage and working capital. The after tax net present value represents the net worth of the lease and the residual economic rent to the resource.

For the Indian leasing system, the net revenue calculations are bypassed and a separate subroutine is called to perform the calculations for the production sharing contracts. The model calculates the contractor's share of cost and profit oil and the government production share in each year. Indian taxes (the maximum amount creditable on American taxes), unadjusted American taxes, and net American taxes are also calculated. After tax net present value is the present value of the contractor's cost and profit oil minus the present value of investment and taxes.

Once the after tax net present value is determined for a particular q_0, other output variables associated with that ATNPV are stored. The model then checks to determine if all q_0s or T values have been evaluated. If not, the model returns to the beginning of the q_0–T loop and repeats the procedure outlined above. If all possible T values or all input q_0 values have been evaluated, the model then proceeds to select the optimal q_0–T combination for this Monte Carlo iteration. The optimal set is the one with the highest ATNPV. This optimal ATNPV is then compared with the potential tax write-off calculated earlier during the exploration phase. If the ATNPV is greater than the potential tax write-off, the optimal ATNPV value is stored as the result for this iteration. If the potential tax write-off from not developing the lease is greater than the potential gain from developing the lease (ATNPV), the decision is made not to develop the lease and the exploration loss is entered into the after tax net present value register. A zero is entered into the register for other output variables such as production, production time horizon, profit share, royalty, and tax. This result corresponds to the real world situation in which some quantity of resource is discovered during the exploration phase, but the economics dictate that the quantity is so small that it is not commercial and the lease is not developed.

Monte Carlo results and model outputs

With the final values of all output variables determined for this Monte Carlo iteration the model then checks to see if all Monte Carlo iterations specified have been completed. If not, the model returns to the beginning of the Monte Carlo simulation and repeats the entire process. If all the Monte Carlo iterations have been completed, then the mean, standard deviation, and other statistics on each output variable are calculated. If desired, histograms can be constructed for after tax net present value (ATNPV) and reserves. The histograms illustrate the distribution of output for these two variables. The distribution of after tax net present value provides the range of potential outcomes and the frequency with which each outcome occurs.

In the above described model, economic rent is composed of royalty and profit share payments, tax payments, and the after tax net present value (ATNPV). These rent components can be manipulated to determine expected bidding behavior and associated impacts for various leasing policy alternatives. For example, in a bonus bidding system with a fixed royalty rate, the expected bonus bid is a function of after tax net present value.[19] The sum of the bonus bid, royalty income, and taxes is equal to total government revenue.[20]

19. Actual bonus bids are a result of bidding strategies formulated from game theoretic approaches combined with bidders estimates of lease value.

20. In the Indian system, economic rent consists of the present value of the government production share plus the cost and profit oil shares of the leaseholder minus the present value of investment and operating costs. Under most circumstances no foreign or domestic taxes are actually paid in the Indian system.

Under a royalty bid system, the winning bid would be expected to be the one that eliminates after tax net present value. In other words, when after tax net present value is constrained to equal zero, royalty payments and taxes alone would compose economic rent, and the royalty bid rate can be determined. Hence, the discounted value of cumulative royalty payments and taxes equals the anticipated economic rent.

One of the policy options programmed into the model is the ability to determine what the royalty bid rate would be under the above assumptions. In addition to the fixed royalty and royalty bid options, a sliding scale royalty system is also incorporated into the model. Under this system, the royalty rate in each period is a function of the production or value of production in that period. This system attempts to capture economies of scale and prevent early termination of production by increasing the royalty rate when production (or value) is high and decreasing the rate when production (or value) is low. Similarly a variable rate profit share system is incorporated into the model which allows the profit share rate to vary in each production period with the amount of profit in that period.

A number of other profit share systems also are included in the model. A capital recovery system, which provides for recovery of capital at a specified rate of interest over a predetermined time period before the government takes its profit share, is one of the profit share variations. Also, a profit share system based on the British profit share plan is included.

Model summary

Clearly a wide range of leasing policy options including bonus bidding systems, royalty systems, profit share systems, the Indian production sharing system and a number of combinations of these systems and their many variants may be analyzed with the generalized leasing model. In addition to the wide range of leasing policy options, a number of tax policy options are also included in the model. In addition, a number of general policy options such as price subsidies, purchase quarantees, price supports, investment subsidies and other policy options designed to increase certainty for private investors are included in the model. Furthermore, other tax policy, general policy, or leasing policy options can easily be incorporated in the model framework. Hence, the model is ideally suited for analysis of a wide range of government policy options dealing with the disposition of publically owned natural resources.

Outputs of the basic model include statistics on the following variables: production time horizon, installed capacity, present value of royalty payments, present value of depletion, present value of taxes and taxable income, present value of profit share or production share payments, production, reserves, present value of investment and operating cost, after tax net present value, and the present value of total production. Additional outputs are provided for specialized leasing or other policy options such as the royalty bidding system.

The use of Monte Carlo simulation with uncertain variables provides an additional dimension to government policy analysis. Not only can the change in expected value of model outputs be determined when a policy variable is changed, but also the change in variance of the model outputs can be determined. Also, because several of the model operations involve non-linear transformations, the results may be different from values obtained using only mean input values. The simulation process more closely approximates the decision making procedure used in the private sector when evaluating potential resource investments.

In the Indian context, the most useful application of the generalized leasing model is to compare the Indian production sharing leasing system with systems in use or proposed for adoption in other parts of the world. Results of this analysis are described in the next section.

ANALYTICAL RESULTS

Using the leasing model described above, the Indian leasing system was compared with the following alternative systems:

1. US bonus bidding system.
2. Annuity capital recovery profit share system.
3. British type profit share system.
4. Variable rate royalty system.
5. Peruvian leasing system.

The profit share systems were tested with both fixed and variable profit share rates. The profit share and variable rate royalty systems were selected for the analysis because they achieved superior results in earlier studies.[21] The Peruvian and US systems were selected to provide a basis of comparison with

21. Kalter, Tyner, and Hughes, pp. 93-111.

systems currently in use in other countries.[22] The Indian leasing system was modeled as described above using the Reading and Bates contract as a guideline. The other systems may be described as follows:

1. *U.S. bonus bidding system:* This system is a bonus bidding system in which the winner is the company with the highest sealed bonus bid. The government collects a royalty of 16.67 percent on all production. Lease terms are for five years renewable if a commercial discovery is made.
2. *Annuity capital recovery profit share:* This system (developed at Cornell) uses the bonus bidding mechanism but relies more heavily on contingency payments. Total initial capital investment plus interest is converted into an annuity at 8 percent interest over an eight year period. The value of this annuity is subtracted from the profit share base before any profit share is taken. The system was tested using a fixed rate of 50 percent and a variable rate structure. For the variable rate structure, the rate ranges from 20 percent to 80 percent. The minimum rate of 20 percent applies in any year in which net income (the profit share base) is up to $10 million. The rate increases 1 percent for each $2 million of annual profits up to a maximum of 80 percent. For example, annual net profits of $40 million would result in a profit share rate of 35 percent.
3. *British type capital recovery system:* This system also is modeled to use a bonus bid with profit share contingency payments. The initial capital investment for exploration and development is multiplied by a factor (1.75 was used in this analysis) to get an investment recovery amount which is deducted from the profit share base before any government profit share is taken. Both a fixed rate of 50 percent and the variable rate structure described above were used in this analysis.
4. *Variable rate royalty system:* This system also uses a cash bonus bid variable with royalty contingency payments. The royalty rate in each period was structured to vary with the value of production in that period. Initially, the rate was set to vary between 5 and 50 percent. The 5 percent level applies to annual production value of up to $10 million. The rate increased 1 percent for each additional $5 million value of annual production. For example, if the annual value of production were $100 million, the applicable royalty rate would be 23 percent.
5. *Peruvian leasing system:* The Peruvian leasing system is a fixed royalty system with a royalty rate between 50 and 56 percent. It has exploration turn back provisions similar to the Indian system. Also, taxes on the pri-

22. The 'British type system' is similar to, but not exactly the same, as a leasing system which has been used in the United Kingdom.

vate contractors are assessed by the Peruvian government and paid by Petroperu for the contractor as in the Indian situation. Hence, American companies would be subject to little or no American tax on their earnings from Peru. For this analysis a 53 percent royalty rate was used.[23]

Assumptions and data inputs

Table 25 gives the common input values for variables which were used in these tests. The values which change by lease system were provided in the system description.

Table 25. Common input values for leasing policy analysis.

Geologic	
Production decline rate, A	0.10
Beta (recovery factor), β	0.0
Reserve distributions	lognormal
Chance of no resource being found	0.4
Price related	
Original oil price, P_o	11.50
Original gas price, GP_o	0.0
Mean of oil price change distribution, *P1M*	0.0
Std. dev. of price change distribution, *PSD*	0.04
Mean of gas price change distribution, *S1M*	0.0
Std. dev. of price change distribution, *SSD*	0.0
Tax related	
Depreciation method, NDEPR	Sum of Years Digits
Depreciation lifetime, N	11 years
Percent investment salvageable, α	10%
Investment tax credit rate, Ω	10%
Federal corporate tax rate, Φ	48%
Indian average tax rate, TAXFR	73%
Time related	
Minimum production time, TMIN	11 years
Cost related	
Working capital factor, WCF	0.1

23. Petroperu, *Peruvian Petroleum: Present and Future 1975.* Edited by Petróleos del Perú, 1975, pp. 25-30.

Table 25 continued

Triangular investment and operating cost contingency distributions	
BMIN, KMIN	0.2
BMODE, KMODE	0.1
BMAX, KMAX	0.3
Rent per acre, RENT	0.0
Investment cost allocation during development, FD	
year 1	0.0
year 2	0.1
year 3	0.2
year 4	0.3
year 5	0.2
year 6	0.2
Percent investment each year that is tangible, TD	
year 1	0.0
year 2	0.5
year 3	0.6
year 4	0.7
year 5	0.8
year 6	0.8
Exploration cost allocation during exploration, FX	
year 1	0.6
year 2	0.4
Percent exploration cost tangible each year, TX	
year 1	0.0
year 2	0.0
Other factors [a]	
Discount rate, R	.12
No. of exploratory wells per 1000 acres, WELLS	.107
No. of acres per tract, ACRES	28,000,000
Bonus factor, BFAC	0.0
No. of MC iterations, NLOOP	200

[a]All of the following variables were set equal to zero: SUB, BCON, θ, z, GPMIN, BYPRCD, ALAMB, CHALMB, ST, NQO, PMIN, MPI, SUBI, MCR.

A power curve cost function was used to calculate investment cost for each reserve value. The curve is of the form shown in equation (20):

(20) $$C = aR^b$$

where R is reserves, C is cost per unit of installed capacity, and a and b the equation coefficients.[24] For this analysis a was set equal to 296,472 and b to

24. This approach to cost estimation by reservoir size was developed in earlier work done by the author. See Kalter, Tyner, and Hughes, pages 80-92 for more details.

−.57958. The corresponding cost estimates are comparable to costs in 200 meters of water in the Gulf of Mexico or the Pacific off Southern California.[25] The assumed cost per exploratory well was $3.1 million.

The alternative systems were evaluated for three different expected reservoir sizes:

	Million barrels	
	Mean	Standard deviation
Small	11.7	5.8
Medium	70.0	49.0
Large	155.8	155.8

These sizes correspond to assumed expected reserve sizes for the Central and Western Gulf of Mexico of the United States.[26]

Several of the data assumptions listed in Table 25 are particularly important. First, a uniform production decline rate of 10 percent was assumed for all tests. Clearly, this assumption is not generally valid. However, in the absence of better information, it was considered the best alternative and representative of average conditions. Second, the *mean* of the annual price change distribution was set equal to zero. This assumption implies that the *expected real* price would not change through time (although the actual sample prices would). Third, a development lag of six years, including a two year exploration period, was assumed for all tests. Although the development period would probably fall through time as activity proceeded in a given region, we have no way of estimating the rate or extent of the change, so uniform development and exploration periods were assumed.

Simulation results

The alternative leasing systems may be evaluated using several criteria. First, we want to learn how effective the system employed by the Government of India is in capturing economic rent as compared with systems used (or proposed for use) by other governments. In other words, we want to learn if the Indian system, as operated in India, is more or less effective than the

25. Industry personnel indicated this was the best basis for estimating costs. Sensitivity tests with higher cost estimates revealed that the trend of the results was essentially unchanged.
26. There is no particular significance to these reserve values. They were selected merely to provide a consistent basis of comparison of the leasing systems. See Kalter, Tyner, and Hughes, pages 5-35, for discussion on reserves and expected field sizes.

American system as operated in the United States. Second, we need to compare all the alternative systems (as they would be operated in India) with the current Indian system to determine which system(s) is most effective in the Indian context. Third, it is desirable to compare the extent of risk sharing between the public and private sectors for the alternative systems.

The first comparison is on the basis of the share of present value of revenue which is (or would be) collected by the respective governments for each system. For systems using the bonus bid, this determination can be made only with assumptions regarding the fraction of after tax net present value which would become the winning bonus bid. To derive this fraction empirically would require knowledge of company risk preference functions, bidding strategies, discount rates, and other factors. In the absence of this information, we will assume that the winning bonus bid would be between 50 and 75 percent of the after tax net present value. Given the bidding history in the U.S. Gulf of Mexico, this range is appropriate, although some bids may have been discounted to a greater extent.[27] For the Peruvian and Indian systems the bonus payment is fixed by the contract and is quite small relative to other systems.

Table 26 displays the simulation results for large and medium reservoirs assuming the bonus bid is 50 to 75 percent of the after tax net present value. The small reservoir analysis resulted in no development under all systems (the field is uneconomic). Table 26 includes economic outputs (ATNPV, tax, royalty, profit share, chance of a less than normal profit), physical outputs (production, installed capacity, production time horizon), cost values, expected gross revenue, and government and private shares of expected present value of revenue.[28] Government revenue is the expected bonus payment plus the present value of tax, royalty, and profit share payments. The cost share is the sum of investment and operating cost as a percentage of revenue (present values). The private profit share is the residual private value divided by the present value of revenue.

For the medium reservoir, the government share ranges from a low of 55 percent for the Peruvian system to a high of 65 percent for the Indian system. Expected present value of gross revenue was highest for the capital recovery profit share systems. This result occurred because more small fields are profitable using these systems (the chance of a less than normal profit is lower). The cost share was 30 or 31 percent for all systems except the variable

27. For a detailed discussion of the factors which enter the bonus bid formation process, see Kalter, Tyner, and Hughes, pp. 41-54.

28. The chance of a less than normal profit is the chance that after tax value is negative using the selected discount rate of 12 percent. This value may be negative because no resources are found or because the discovery is too small to be profitably developed. Use of a lower discount rate (8 percent) did not appreciably change the results.

Table 26. Results of model simulations.

Leasing System	ATNPV (P.V.- mil. $)	Tax (P.V.- mil. $)	Royalty (P.V.- mil. $)	Profit Share (P.V.- mil. $)	Chance of a Less Than Normal Profit (%)	Exp. Prod. (mil. bbl.)
Reserve Size = 70 Million Barrels						
Indian	5.8	0	0	69.4	57	32.7
U.S. Cash Bonus	30.8	29.1	19.4	0	50	35.1
Annuity Capital Recovery						
Fixed Rate	20.9	21.4	0	37.6	49	35.5
Variable Rate	31.0	28.8	0	20.5	48	35.8
British Type Cap. Recovery						
Fixed Rate	22.2	22.3	0	35.6	48	35.7
Variable Rate	30.9	28.7	0	20.6	48	35.8
Variable Royalty Rate = 5-50%	24.3	29.3	24.1	0	42	36.9
Peruvian	15.0	0	57.4	0	56	32.9
Reserve Size = 155.8 Million Barrels						
Indian	21.9	0	0	178.7	47	77.2
U.S. Cash Bonus	85.5	70.4	41.7	0	51	75.5
Annuity Capital Recovery						
Fixed Rate	58.2	49.1	0	91.9	50	76.3
Variable Rate	67.8	54.6	0	68.8	49	76.4
British Type Cap. Recovery						
Fixed Rate	60.4	50.7	0	88.0	50	76.3
Variable Rate	66.9	53.9	0	69.8	49	76.4
Variable Royalty Rate = 5-50%	50.3	54.9	87.3	0	42	78.6
Peruvian	63.1	0	135.0	0	47	77.2

royalty systems. Cost share was slightly higher for this system because the present value of revenue is somewhat lower. The variable royalty rate schedule provides an incentive to stretch out production and revenue to achieve a lower effective overall royalty rate. Even though the variable royalty rate system achieves the lowest chance of a less than normal profit (more small fields are developed), present value of revenue is reduced because the production time horizon is longer.

Table 26 continued.

Instl. Cap. (mil. bbl.)	Prod. Time Horizon (years)	Dev. Cost Given Discovery (P.V.- mil. $)	Exp. Total Cost (P.V.- mil. $)	Exp. Gross Revenue (P.V.- mil. $)	Govt. Share of Present Value of Revenue (%)	Cost Share of Present Value of Revenue (%)	Private Profit Share of Present Value Revenue (%)	Total Private Share of Present Value Revenue (%)
8.8	11.2	72.7	31.6	106.8	65	30	6	35
8.2	11.0	70.7	35.4	114.6	56-62	31	7-13	38-44
8.1	11.0	70.1	36.1	116.0	60-64	31	5-9	36-40
8.0	11.0	69.6	36.5	116.8	55-62	31	7-13	38-44
8.1	11.0	69.8	36.3	116.4	59-64	31	5-10	36-41
8.0	11.0	69.5	36.5	116.7	55-62	31	7-13	38-44
6.9	12.3	63.5	36.8	114.4	57-63	32	5-11	37-43
8.6	11.8	71.0	31.2	103.5	55	30	14	44
7.1	11.1	100.2	53.1	253.7	70	21	9	30
8.1	11.0	103.9	50.9	248.5	62-71	20	9-17	29-37
7.7	11.0	102.7	51.9	251.0	68-74	21	6-12	27-33
6.6	11.5	99.9	51.0	242.2	65-72	21	7-14	28-35
7.7	11.0	102.7	51.9	251.0	67-73	21	6-12	27-33
6.6	11.6	99.7	50.9	241.5	65-72	21	7-14	28-35
4.4	13.1	89.1	52.1	244.7	68-74	21	5-10	26-31
2.0	11.3	99.5	52.8	250.8	54	21	25	46

For the large reservoir, the government revenue share ranges from 54 to 74 percent. The Indian system resulted in a 70 percent government share, higher than the lower range of all alternative systems and considerably higher than the Peruvian system. Cost share was 20 or 21 percent for all systems. The chance of a less than normal profit ranged from 42 percent for the variable rate royalty system to 51 percent for the current United States system. The Indian system was second lowest at 47 percent.

Reviewing the results for the medium reservoir, it is clear that the government share for the Indian system is greater than or equal to the highest government share for any of the other systems tested. The Peruvian system ranked lowest by this criterion, and the U.S. system ranked behind the other alternative systems. For the large reservoir, the Indian system was not clearly superior to the capital recovery or variable royalty systems. Government share for these systems depends on the bonus bidding strategy. The present value of the government share of expected gross revenue was highest for the Indian system. Overall, the Indian system achieved results equivalent or superior to all the other alternative systems.

In one respect, the Indian and Peruvian systems fared poorly compared to the other systems. Because of the high royalty and production shares taken by these systems, small fields could not be economically developed. In fact, the smallest field that could be economically developed for either system was about forty million barrels. If costs were higher, this minimum developable field size would be even larger. In the Indian context, the implication of this result is that small fields would not be developed by the private contractor and would be turned back to the Oil and Natural Gas Commission for future development. This result may not be unsatisfactory from the viewpoint of the Indian government because the government may be more interested in achieving rapid development of large fields, and quite willing to postpone development of smaller fields into the future. This result also corresponds with industry expectations since as one industry spokesman put it, 'These contracts are designed for development of large fields only; small fields cannot be produced profitably under the terms of the leasing contracts.'[29] Although this result may be acceptable to the Indian government, it should be considered in establishing future leasing strategy.

The second step in evaluating the Indian leasing system is to compare it with the other systems in the Indian context. The major change required is to assume that the contingency payments for the capital recovery and variable royalty systems could be labeled taxes and that no American (or other corporate home government) taxes would be payable. In addition the variable rate structures and fixed rates must be raised to compensate for elimination of taxes. In the Indian context the Peruvian and American systems would be essentially equivalent (both are fixed rate royalty systems), so there is no need to include them in the second test.

Table 27 displays the results of this second test for the large reservoir. The fixed rate capital recovery systems were simulated with a 95 percent profit

29. Interview with an industry spokesman (off the record).

share rate and the variable rate range was from 90 to 98 percent. For this reservoir, the capital recovery systems performed better than the Indian system capturing from 72 to 77 percent of the present value of revenue as compared with 70 percent for the Indian system. A smaller percentage of the discoveries were uneconomic using capital recovery systems.[30] Cost share was essentially unchanged from the previous test. Private profit share of gross revenue ranged from 2 to 6 percent for the capital recovery systems as compared with 9 percent for the Indian system. On pure economic criteria, the capital recovery systems appeared somewhat superior to the Indian system for the large reservoir. Similar results were achieved for the medium reservoir.

The variable royalty system was also tested with a higher (20-80 percent) and more rapidly accelerating rate structure and no tax payments. When the higher rate structure was applied, this created an incentive to reduce installed capacity and increase production time horizon.[31] By spreading out production over time, the company could achieve a lower royalty rate in each period; or conversely, the most profitable production scale would entail lower capacity and a lengthened production time horizon. The longer production time caused the present value of revenue to fall significantly. Therefore, the variable royalty system could not achieve results superior to the current Indian system.

The third basis of comparison of alternative systems is on the difference in risk sharing among systems. One measure of risk is the standard deviation/mean ratio of output variables. Table 28 displays these ratios for the results of the systems test in the Indian setting. The government share for the Indian system and all the capital recovery systems had ratios of 1.6 and the variable royalty system 2.0. The government would accept a greater degree of risk with the variable royalty system than the others. Conversely, the private sector must accept a greater amount of risk with the capital recovery systems, particularly those with variable rates.

30. Forty-one percent of the Monte Carlo iterations produced no resource discovery. Hence, a 42 percent chance of a less than normal profit means that only 1 percent of the situations represent discovered but uneconomic fields.

31. For the structure shown, the time horizon increased from 11.1 years for the Indian system to 16.1 years for the variable royalty system without achieving a higher ATNPV. With an even higher structure, the time horizon increased to 17 years and the present value of revenue fell significantly.

Table 27. Model simulations in the Indian setting.

Leasing System	ATNPV (P.V.- mil. $)	Profit Share or Royalty (P.V.- mil. $)	Chance of a Less Than Normal Profit (%)	Exp. Prod. (mil. bbl.)	Prod. Time Horizon (years)
Indian	21.9	178.7	47	77.2	11.1
Annuity Capital Recovery					
Fixed Rate[a]	8.9	191.4	45	78.0	11.0
Variable Rate[b]	4.3	193.3	42	78.4	12.2
British Type Cap. Recovery					
Fixed Rate[a]	16.4	184.6	42	78.4	11.0
Variable Rate[b]	11.4	189.7	42	78.4	11.0
Variable Royalty Rate[c]	56.7	112.5	42	78.6	16.1

[a]The fixed rate for capital recovery systems was 95 percent.
[b]The variable rate for capital recovery systems ranged from 90 to 98 percent.
[c]The variable royalty rate ranged from 20 to 80 percent.

Table 28. Standard deviation-mean ratios for alternative systems.

	System	After tax net present value	Profit or production share
1.	Indian	1.8	1.6
2.	Annuity capital recovery		
	– fixed rate	2.6	1.6
	– variable rate	3.3	1.6
3.	British type capital recovery		
	– fixed rate	1.9	1.6
	– variable rate	2.0	1.6
4.	Variable royalty	1.2	2.0

Exp. Total Cost (P.V.- mil. $)	Exp. Gross Revenue (P.V.- mil. $)	Govt. Share of Present Value of Revenue (%)	Cost Share of Present Value of Revenue (%)	Private Profit Share of Present Value Revenue (%)	Total Private Share of Present Value Revenue (%)
53.1	253.7	70	21	9	30
54.4	254.7	75	21	3	24
53.9	251.5	77	21	2	23
55.4	256.4	72	22	6	28
55.4	256.5	74	22	4	26
48.2	217.4	51	22	27	49

SUMMARY

Based on this analysis, what system should the government of India use? The answer is unclear. With each system modeled in its own institutional setting, the Indian system appears to be superior to the other alternatives. In other words, currently the Government of India is doing a better job of collecting economic rent than the other countries evaluated.

However, when proposed capital recovery systems are compared with the Indian system in an Indian institutional setting, the capital recovery systems appear somewhat better. This conclusion should be qualified for four main reasons.

First, all three systems – Indian, annuity capital recovery, and British type capital recovery – are capital recovery profit share systems. They are all structured to allow cost recovery plus a return to capital. In that sense, they all approach a pure economic profit share because a return to capital is allowed. In the Indian system, the return to capital is allowed by permitting recovery of three times the original cost through cost oil and profit oil. In the annuity capital recovery, the return is accounted for in calculating the annuity, and in British type capital recovery, 1.75 times the original investment is recovered before a profit share is taken. The differences among the three systems have more to do with the rate levels and structures than differences in theoretical rationale. It is quite possible that changes in the rates or slight structural changes (as in the Asamera contract) would make the Indian system perform as well as the other capital recovery systems.

A second qualification concerns institutional issues. Companies operating in Asia are familar with the Indian-Indonesian type of system and may be hesitant to accept other systems. Also, companies may not accept the high risk and low profit potential associated with the other capital recovery systems.

Third, with respect to the British type system, the feature allowing all oil during early production years (until 1.75 times cost is recovered) to go to the private contractor may not be acceptable to the Government of India. India needs oil quickly and may prefer a system which allows cost recovery over a longer period of time.

Fourth, the United States and other foreign governments may not allow profit share payments under the other capital recovery systems to be counted as taxes. The Government of India would have to devise a procedure to eliminate foreign tax liability in order to attract foreign companies.

The basic conclusion of this research is that India should use one of the capital recovery profit share systems; either its current system or one of the suggested modifications.[32] Through use of one of these systems, the Indian government can assure development of all major oil fields, retain a large portion of the oil for itself, and undertake no risk nor make any capital investment.

Furthermore, by taking advantage of tax provisions in the U.S. tax codes for crediting foreign taxes, the Indian government is able to effect a real resource transfer from foreign taxpayers (currently U.S. and Canadian) to domestic taxpayers.[33] When the Indian system was simulated on an expected large reservoir with no Indian taxes (to offset American taxes), the level of development dropped significantly and the government's production share fell from $178.7 million to $160.0 million. If two large fields were to be discovered in each of three leasing areas, this resource transfer from foreign to Indian taxpayers would amount to more than $100 million (present value).

32. Neither of the alternative capital recovery systems are currently in use today. The British type system is a modification of a system formerly used by Great Britain.

33. Recently the Internal Revenue Service ruled that these 'tax payments' would no longer be creditable on American taxes. However, the general concensus among both industry and U.S. government officials is that this ruling will not become binding and will be nullified either by legislation, tax treaties, or new rulings.

POLICY RECOMMENDATIONS

Based on this analysis, it appears that it is to the advantage of the government of India to continue to lease offshore areas to foreign companies using the current system or a similar capital recovery system. Some of the advantages of the system have been described above. Continued leasing increases the possibility of a very large or giant discovery. To determine what would result from such a discovery, the system was simulated with an expected reserve find of 1.85 billion barrels. The results are rather dramatic:

1. Initial production (after a development build up) could amount to 216 million barrels (27.8 million tons) per year which would be more than adequate to replace all Indian imports of crude oil.
2. The present value of the government's share from such a discovery would be about $4.5 billion, and the government would have taken no risk nor made any capital investment to achieve this return.

Similar results could be achieved from discovery of several smaller fields.

The Indian leasing system offers institutional as well as economic advantages. By leasing areas to different companies India should not experience the previous problems of foreign domination of the petroleum industry. The leases granted thus far have been to non-integrated relatively small petroleum exploration companies. According to the lease provisions, India maintains complete control over domestic refining and marketing and has access to all the petroleum produced. The lease provisions also provide a strong incentive for the lease-holders to develop the resources, take their share of the oil in the early years, and not become entrenched in the Indian economy.

The basic conclusion of this analysis, then, is that the Indian leasing system is very good, and that leasing should proceed rapidly to accelerate development of India's petroleum resources and ameliorate the ill effects of oil imports on foreign exchange.

5. Electric power

Electric power is one of the most important components of the energy sector. The correlation between power consumption and the index of industrial production in India for the years 1955-56 through 1970-71 was .96. The close relationship between power consumption and industrial production is apparent. However, power production and consumption are also vital for the agricultural sector. The average annual rate of growth of consumption of electric power in the agricultural sector from 1953-54 to 1970-71 was 20.2 percent as compared with 12.0 percent for the mining and manufacturing sectors and 10.5 percent for the domestic sector.[1]

In his work on an employment-oriented strategy of development focusing on increased agricultural production, John Mellor calls for a higher rate of growth of power than in previous years:

> It seems likely that an employment-oriented program of development will require a much faster growth rate of electric power. That accelerated growth will claim a substantial proportion of the investment resources available to the public sector, and make even more difficult the allocation of funds to other capital intensive industries. Indeed, the distribution of capital to those industries is likely to starve the power sector, ensure the failure of agricultural and labor intensive industries, and, as a result of that deficiency, guarantee a foreign-exchange gap.[2]

RECENT POWER SHORTAGES

In recent years power shortages have been a problem for both the industrial and agricultural sectors. P. M. Agerwala observed that 'Power shortages seemed to have added a new dimension to the ideological differences over granting priorities to industry and agriculture. In one state, power supplies were being stopped specifically for providing interim relief either to industry

1. V. P. Chitale and Mrs. M. Roy, *Energy Crisis in India* (New Delhi: Economic and Scientific Research Foundation, 1975), p. 21.
2. John W. Mellor, *The New Economics of Growth* (Ithaca: Cornell University Press, 1976), p. 123.

or to agriculture at the cost of the other.'[3] During 1974-75, power cuts ranged from 25 percent in Maharashtra to 60 percent in Tamil Nadu, Punjab, Haryana, and Delhi.[4] Table 29 shows the states and regions which experienced severe power shortages in 1974-75. The power situation in India was quite troublesome during the last three years of the Fourth Plan (1972- 1974). There were serious disruptions of production in a number of areas and industries. Table 30 shows percentage changes in production for several important industries from the first eight months of 1972 to the same period in 1974.

Table 29. Regions and states seriously affected by power shortages 1974-75.

REGION	DATE September 1974	May 1975	September 1975
Northern	Haryana Punjab Uttar Pradesh	Haryana Punjab Uttar Pradesh Jammu and Kashmir	Uttar Pradesh
Western	Gujarat Maharashtra	Gujarat Maharashtra Madhya Pradesh	Maharashtra
Southern	Andhra Pradesh Tamil Nadu Karnataka	Andhra Pradesh Tamil Nadu Karnataka	Karnataka
Eastern	West Bengal	West Bengal Bihar	West Bengal
North- Eastern	Assam	Assam	Assam

Source: World Bank working papers, 1976.

Although there has been loss of production due to power outages in each of these industries, the importance of this factor in the total production change cannot be conclusively established. The aluminum industry is heavily dependent on electric power and the loss in production is largely attributable to the power shortage. Power shortages in West Bengal have seriously affected the production of jute textiles. In the cases of cement and steel, the production loss was due to shortages of coal as well as the shortage of electric power. Even

3. *Economic Times* (1-31-75), quoted in Mellor, p. 123.
4. Sham Lal, p. 609.

though the nitrogenous fertilizer capacity increased significantly over this period, production remained relatively constant primarily because of the power shortage.[5]

Table 30. Percentage changes in production in selected industries for the period January-August 1972 to 1974.

INDUSTRY	% CHANGE
Aluminum[a]	-32.4
Jute textiles[b]	-23.3
Cotton yarn[c]	-5.5
Cotton fabrics[c]	-6.4
Cement[b]	-12.5
Ingot steel[d]	-6.9
Nitrogenous fertilizers	+0.7

Source: Henderson, p. 99; taken from *Monthly Review of the Indian Economy*, and Fertilizer Association of India.

[a]Figures are for January-June 1972 to 1974.
[b]Production of firms which account for at least 90 percent of total production.
[c]Production of the mill sector only.
[d]Includes production of the major steel plants which account for 85 percent of total production.

There are numerous reasons why the power shortages occurred. During the Fourth Plan, only one half of the planned additions to generating capacity were actually completed (4.6 of 9.3 million kilowatts). Cost escalations for new power plants were a major reason for the slippage in development plans. Poor plant maintenance is another reason for the power shortage. For thermal plants in India, the utilization rate has averaged about 47 percent. Lack of preventive maintenance and difficulty in obtaining imported spare parts are the primary reasons for the low utilization factor.[6] A further cause of the shortage is high transmission losses. Such losses are about 17 percent for India as compared with less than 10 percent for most developed countries such as West Germany – 6 percent, France – 7 percent, and Austria – 10 percent.[7]

From this brief introduction to the current power situation in India, it is clear that electric power is very important for increases in both industrial and agricultural production. Equally clear is the critical situation with respect to power supplies that India has faced since 1972 and to a lesser extent for many

5. Henderson, p. 98.
6. G.o.I., *Draft: Fifth Plan*, 2: 117-18; Henderson, p. 101.
7. G.o.I., *Fuel Policy Committee*, pp. 78-79.

years. This chapter provides a look at the power sector as a whole and then at the individual sources of electric power: hydropower and thermal (coal and nuclear) power. Finally, the progress of rural electrification is reviewed and related to the general power situation in India.

FORECASTING POWER DEMAND AND GENERATING CAPACITY REQUIREMENTS

To forecast the amount of installed capacity needed at some future time, the first step is to forecast the anticipated energy consumption for that time. This forecast is often made using the close relationship between energy consumption and national income described in Chapter 1. Forecasts of national income (in India) are the agreed upon targets of income growth established in the five year plans. Hence, to determine the expected energy consumption at the end of a plan period, the expected income at that time is used in a regression model to forecast energy consumption. This process is described in somewhat more detail below.

Terms used in describing electric power

Before continuing into more detail on electric power supply in India, it will be useful to define some terms commonly used in discussing and analyzing electric power. Generally, the terms and definitions used in India are similar to those used in the United States. However, it is difficult to derive a consistent set of definitions that is compatible with all data sources. The definitions provided below are generally consistent with procedures in use in India today.

Installed capacity of a plant or system is the maximum continuous capacity (kilowatts) of the generating equipment. System capacity is normally calculated at the end of each fiscal year.

Peak capability is the maximum reasonable peak generating capacity of the existing system at a given time. Installed capacity and peak capability are different because plant capacity may diminish over time (primarily thermal stations), and the peak capacity of hydro stations may occur at a time other than the time of system peak load. In India, peak capability has ranged from 85 to 93 percent of installed capacity with 90 percent being used for forecasting purposes.[8]

Peak load of a power system is the 'Maximum simultaneous ultimate customer demand within the supply area of the system' when no restriction is

8. Ibid., pp. 80-81.

imposed on power consumption.[9] The ratio between peak load and peak capability is termed the demand factor. The margin between peak load and peak capability provides for scheduled maintenance, emergency outages, and operating requirements of the power system.[10] The demand factor used for forecasting purposes is .8. The ratio of the energy demand per year and the peak load multiplied by the number of hours in a year (8760) is known as the load factor and is shown in equation (21):

$$(21) \qquad \text{Load factor} = \frac{\text{energy demand/year (kwh)}}{\text{peak load (kw)} \times 8760}$$

The load factor used for forecasting purposes in India (and in the United States) is 60 percent.[11]

Forecasting relationships

Energy consumption must be adjusted for energy losses to determine total energy requirement. In recent years power transmission and distribution losses in India have ranged from 14 to 17 percent. Table 31 shows the power losses as a percentage of power available for transmission and per capita power consumption in each state in a recent year. Although losses have generally been somewhat higher, a loss figure of 13.8 percent is used in converting projected energy consumption to projected energy requirement as shown in equation (22):

$$(22) \qquad \text{Energy requirement} = \frac{\text{energy consumption}}{.862}$$

Using the process and factors described above, the forecast of energy requirement can be converted to the total required amount of installed capacity. Subtracting existing capacity, the new installed capacity required for the plan period can be calculated as shown in equation (23);

$$(23) \qquad \text{Installed capacity} = \frac{\text{energy requirement (kwh)}}{\text{capability factor} \times \text{demand factor} \times \text{load factor} \times 8760}$$

9. Central Electricity Authority, *Ninth Annual Electric Power Survey of India* (Delhi: Government of India Press, 1975), p. 11.

10. The Central Electricity Authority (p. 11) does not separate the demand factor and capability factor. The term peak availability is used to account for both capacity diminution and maintenance requirements. In that case an availability factor of .72 (.8 × .9) would be used for forecasting purposes.

11. G.o.I., *Fuel Policy Committee*, p. 80.

Table 31. Per capita power consumption and power losses by state.

State	Per Capita Consumption (1971-72) Gwh	Power Losses (1970-71) %
Andhra Pradesh	57	24.8
Assam	25	17.9
Bihar	65	23.6
Gujarat	140	16.6
Haryana	111	27.9
Jammu and Kashmir	40	21.5
Karnataka	115	14.3
Kerala	74	12.2
Madhya Pradesh	58	14.4
Maharashtra	168	13.1
Orissa	97	5.5
Punjab	169	35.5
Rajasthan	53	11.9
Tamil Nadu	135	17.2
Uttar Pradesh	60	23.6
West Bengal	115	8.3
All India	94	17.3

Sources: Consumption-Henderson, p. 77; Power losses- *Report of the Fuel Policy Committee*, p. 79.

The values currently being used for forecasting in India are substituted into equation (23) in equation (24):

$$(24) \qquad \text{Installed capacity} = \frac{\text{energy requirement (kwh)}}{.9 \times .8 \times .6 \times 8760} = \frac{\text{energy requirement (kwh)}}{.432 \times 8760}$$

Hence, the anticipated energy requirement divided by 3784.3 yields the required installed capacity.[12]

12. The term plant factor is the product of the load factor (.6) and the demand factor (.8) and excludes the capability factor (.9). The plant factor, also called a plant utilization factor, refers to the percentage of peak capability which is utilized during a one year period. Plant factors for thermal and hydropower combined have historically been somewhat higher than .48 in India.

Forecasting procedures used in India

Using the relationships outlined above, the amount of installed capacity required for each plan period can be calculated given a forecast for energy demand (consumption) or required energy generation during the plan period. A number of different procedures have been tried to develop reliable forecasts of power generating requirements and power consumption in India. The Central Electricity Authority used three different forecasting methods and took the average of the results as their forecast value. The three methods were trend, end-use, and Scheer's formula.

In the first approach, an exponential trend was calculated using energy requirement data from 1950-51 to 1971-72. The regression equation which resulted is shown in equation (25):

$$(25) \qquad Y = -3411.39 + 8555.05E^{.0988X}$$

where X is time in years with 1950-51 as the beginning year.

With the second approach, the end-use method, the energy consumption of each of the following categories was estimated separately: 1) industrial, 2) domestic, 3) commercial, 4) public lighting, 5) traction, 6) irrigation, and 7) water works and sewage pumping. Consumption of each category is projected based on expected changes in production.

The third approach using Scheer's formula is based on the hypothesis that for every one hundred fold increase in per capita generation, the rate of growth of power generation will be reduced by half. Equation 26 shows the formula which was developed after studying load growth in a number of countries throughout the world including India:

$$(26) \qquad G = \frac{10^C}{U^{.15}}$$

where G is annual percentage growth in power generation, U is per capita generation and C is a constant which is .02 multiplied by the population growth rate plus 1.33. The formula is used iteratively to forecast power consumption growth for each year with the preceding value used to forecast the next year's growth. Each of these forecasting procedures produces a forecast of the energy requirement rather than energy consumption or energy demand. The average forecast energy requirement for 1978-79 produced by the Central Electricity Authority is 133.5 billion kilowatt hours.[13]

13. Central Electricity Authority, *Electric Power Survey*, pp. 46-47.

The Fuel Policy Committee used the regression method correlating national income with electricity consumption, and the end-use method. The regression method was employed primarily as a check on the end-use method which was exercised in generating the estimates actually used by the Fuel Policy Committee. Three different estimates were made with the end-use method: one based on past trends and experience, one incorporating the effects of increased petroleum prices, and one case which is an intermediate level between the other two cases. The first case estimates depended upon three assumptions: 1) that the factors which determine the level and patterns of fuel usage in the past will continue to operate in the future; 2) that the relative prices of energy sources will remain constant; and 3) that technology shifts will continue in the same patterns as in the immediate past. The third case incorporated the assumption that the relative price of oil products and other fuels will continue to be the same as existed in the first quarter of 1974. It also established estimates for the ability to increase fuel efficiency and substitute other fuels for oil products. The consumption forecasts for 1978-79 using the three methods were 97.1, 100.3 and 103.9 billion kilowatt hours. This method was also used to forecast total generation requirements for the same year which were 119.9, 124.0 and 128.0 billion kilowatt hours respectively.[14]

Bias in the forecasting procedures

There is a basic problem with these forecasting procedures when the resulting demand forecasts are used to project desired increases in installed capacity or power generation for planning purposes. This problem is most easily seen using the regression or end-use techniques employed by the Central Electricity Authority and the Fuel Policy Committee. Both regression equations use recent historical power consumption data as the basis for projecting future power consumption. The problem with this approach is that if the power supply were inadequate during the recent past, this same inadequacy will be projected into the future periods. In other words, use of this technique for forecasting future consumption demand amounts to planning for future shortages if shortages existed in the past. The end-use method produces the same result. Production constrained by inadequate power supply leads to forecasts which will perpetuate constraints on production. Since the other forecasting techniques have achieved similar results, the same problem also exists with these techniques.

14. G.o.I., *Fuel Policy Committee*, pp. 11-20.

The forecasting problem really has two components. First, the existence of power outages and power shortages during the base period means that consumption would have been higher with existing demand had the power been available. In other words, the existing base for industrial production, agricultural production, and domestic consumption would have resulted in a higher total power consumption if the supply had been available. Use of this constrained consumption for planning purposes would result in future power shortages because they would be built into the calculated capacity requirements during future planning periods.

Second, and perhaps even more important, as discussed in Chapter 1, the existence or expectation of power shortages leads to a reduction in investment in power intensive industry and agriculture. The potential demand for power is actually much higher than the existing demand level because the consumption base would be much larger if not for the power outages and power shortages which reduce the level of investment. A higher level of investment in power generating capacity and the resulting public assurance of ready availability of power would lead to increases in investment in power consumptive industry and agricultural activities.

For both these reasons, potential energy consumption and the energy requirement during future planning periods would be much higher than either of the forecasts discussed above or the forecasts used as the basis for Fifth Plan investments in power generation. The term *potential power consumption* should be emphasized because, clearly, the *current forecasts can become a self-fulfilling prophecy*. If shortages existed during the base data period, planning capacity additions based on these forecasts will lead to a supply constrained consumption during the planning horizon.

Table 32 displays the range of current forecasts of energy consumption and energy requirement together with the required installed capacity to achieve generation of the stipulated requirement and the calculated growth rate in power generation capacity which would result during the Fifth Plan (1973-74 to 1978-79). Since the Central Electricity Authority forecast is in terms of energy requirement, the required installed capacity can be calculated directly using equation 24. The forecast of 133.5 billion kilowatt hours requires an installed capacity of 35.3 million kilowatts. At the beginning of the Fifth Plan India had 18.9 million kilowatts of installed capacity. These figures result in a rate of growth in power generating capacity during the Fifth Plan of 12.6 percent. The projections used in the *Draft Fifth Five Year Plan* are very similar to those developed by the Central Electricity Authority. Although the plan document calls for an installed capacity of 35.4 million kilowatts at the end of the plan, it also stipulates that one million kilowatts will be retired during the

Table 32. Forecasts of power consumption and requirement and required installed capacity for the Fifth Pla

Source or approach	Forecast energy consump-tion (bil. kwh)	Energy require-ment (bil. kwh)	Required installed capacity (mil. kw)	Growth rate in power generation capacity 1973-74 to 1978-79 (%)
Central Electricity Authority[a]		133.5	35.3	12.6
Draft Fifth Five Year Plan[b]		130.0	35.4	12.6
Adjusted Fifth Plan[c]		130.0	34.4	12.0
Fuel Policy Committee[d]				
1. End-use method II	100.3	124.0	32.8	11.1
2. Above with 13.8% losses	100.3	116.4	30.8	9.8
Estimates derived by increasing Fuel Policy Committee demand forecasts				
1. Increased by 10%	110.3	130.6	34.5	12.1
2. Increased by 20%	120.4	142.4	37.6	13.8
3. Increased by 30%	130.4	154.3	40.8	15.5
4. Increased by 40%	140.4	166.2	43.9	17.0

Sources: Report of the Fuel Policy Committee, p. 20 and pp. 79-81; CEA, *Ninth Annual Electric Power Survey* *India*, 1974; *Draft Fifth Five Year Plan*, Volume II, pp. 117-120.

[a]The forecast was computed in terms of energy requirement.
[b]Although the *Draft Fifth Five Year Plan* is not consistent throughout in terms of energy requirement, this figu appears to be the appropriate one (from Volume II, pp. 117-120). Volume I of the Plan reports an energ requirement of 120 billion kwh.
[c]The actual planned increase in installed capacity during the Fifth Plan is only to 34.4 million kw because on million kw is slated to be retired during the Fifth Plan. Also, 34.4 kw is the calculated required installed capaci using equation 24.
[d]The end-use forecasts are provided on p. 20 of the *Report of the Fuel Policy Committee*; the second forecast given on p. 81.

plan meaning that the actual planned installed capacity at the end of the Fifth Plan would be 34.4 million kilowatts. Because over one million kilowatts of this planned addition will come on line during the last half of the last year of the plan, the actual target for average installed capacity for the last year of the plan is 33 million kilowatts. Power generating capacity would grow at an annual rate of 12.0 or 12.6 percent depending upon which final figure is used in the calculation.[15]

15. G.o.I., *Draft: Fifth Plan*, 2:120.

Table 32 also displays two of the forecasts developed by the Fuel Policy Committee. Using end-use method number two described above, the forecast energy consumption for 1978-79 is 100.3 billion kilowatt hours. Two different values are shown for the corresponding energy requirement for this level of energy consumption. Assuming 13.8 percent losses, the Fuel Policy Committee projects an energy requirement of 116.4 billion kilowatt hours, and using end-use method two, the forecast energy requirement is 124.0 billion kilowatt hours. These values for energy requirement correspond to installed capacities of 30.8 and 32.8 million kilowatts respectively. The resulting growth rates in power generation during the Fifth Plan would be 9.8 and 11.1 percent.

Forecast modifications

Based upon the above discussion of forecasting procedures, these forecasts are too low and should be increased because power consumption was constrained during the base period. Using the Fuel Policy Committee forecast for energy consumption for 1978-79 as a base, Table 32 provides the results when that base is increased by 10, 20, 30, and 40 percent. These increases in the forecast energy consumption will provide an indication of the potential range of required installed capacities to compensate for the downward bias in energy demand forecast. If the Fuel Policy Committee forecast is increased by 10 percent, the resulting energy requirement is 130.6 billion kilowatt hours which is roughly comparable to the forecast used in formulating the *Fifth Five Year Plan*. If the forecast is increased by 20 percent, the energy requirement is 142.4 billion kilowatt hours and the required installed capacity is 37.6 million kilowatts. This would amount to a growth rate in power generating capacity over the Fifth Plan of 13.8 percent. If the base forecast is increased by 30 percent, the resulting energy requirement is 154.3 billion kilowatt hours and the required installed capacity is 40.8 million kilowatts. The growth in power generating capacity over the Fifth Plan becomes 15.5 percent. With an increase of 40 percent, the growth rate in power generating capacity becomes 17.0 percent.

To get an idea of the importance of these adjusted forcasts, we will use the forecast which is increased by 30 percent as an example to calculate the potential increase in the Fifth Plan power allocation which would be required to achieve this result. The Fifth Plan currently calls for 16.548 million kilowatts to be installed during the plan period. The budget for this installation is Rs. 4958.10 crores which amounts to an average of Rs. 299.6 crores per million kilowatts installed. If the installed capacity at the end of the Fifth Plan were increased to 40.8 million kilowatts, an additional 5.4 million kilowatts would have to be installed during the plan. The plan budget for power generation would have to be increased by approximately Rs. 1618 crores which is a 33 percent increase in the budget for power generation and distribution.

Increases of this order of magnitude in expenditures on power generation facilities are needed during the Fifth and Sixth Five Year Plans. This increased level of expenditure results from only a 16 percent increase in the forecast energy requirement by the Central Electricity Authority (since their forecast was already higher than that of the Fuel Policy Committee). It is highly probable that such an increase could be absorbed by the Indian economy and would provide beneficial results in terms of future growth in national income.

There is no special significance attached to the numbers in this example; rather the point is that significant increases in the plan allocation to power generation and distribution facilities are needed to prevent a continuation of the situation of power outages and power shortages which constrain economic growth.

POWER DEVELOPMENT IN INDIA

Power development in India has been primarily the responsibility of the state governments. According to the Indian constitution the responsibility for power development is shared by the central and state governments. However, from the early years, power generation and distribution has been handled primarily by the states. The Electricity Supply Act of 1948 created an Electricity Council in the central government, but provided for state electricity boards which would have control over power generation and distribution.[16] Through time, the central government has taken an increasing role in the power sector, especially in the planning and implementation of large scale hydro projects which concern more than one state.

With encouragement from outside authorities (especially from the World Bank), the central government has also taken a larger role in overseeing the finances of state electricity boards. A government White Paper published in 1967 established the first economic criteria (as opposed to financial criteria) for determining prices of power and acceptable rates of return on investments. It established that price should approximate marginal cost and that investment appraisal should be accomplished using discounted cash flow

16. Venkataraman, p. 113.

techniques. The minimum acceptable rate of retun (discount rate) was initially set at 8 percent, and increased to 10 percent in 1969.[17]

However, despite the encouragement from the Center, the state electricity boards are still not receiving an adequate return on investment. During the Fourth Plan, the rate of return was substantially less than 9 percent, probably less than 5 percent. The Fuel Policy Committee strongly recommended that electricity tariffs be revised in all states in order to achieve a minimum return on investment of 10 percent.[18]

With this overall background, we now turn to power development from each of the three major sources of power: hydropower, coal, and nuclear. We conclude this chapter with a brief look at rural electrification in India.

Hydropower

As was established in Chapter 2, India is well endowed with hydropower resources. As of 1970, less than 18 percent of India's hydropower resources had been developed or were under development.[19] Hydropower is a renewable resource and hydropower development normally also provides benefits in irrigation and flood control. It is widely accepted that India could develop economically at least the 41.2 megawatts of hydropower potential evaluated by the Energy Survey Committee in 1965. Since the cost of alternative energy sources has risen, the real potential is probably higher (see Chapter 2). The question, then, is why has the pace of hydropower development proceeded so slowly?

This question was posed to a number of officials of the Planning Commission, Fuel Policy Committee, Department of Science and Technology, Ministry of Finance, Ministry of Energy (Department of Power), and other agencies.[20] The officials were unanimous in agreeing that the pace of hydropower development had been slow, and they provided a

17. Ibid., pp. 13-24.
18. G.o.I., *Fuel Policy Committee*, p. 103.
19. Ibid., p. 28.
20. The discussion on hydropower development evolved from discussions with the following individuals: Dr. A. Rahman, Council of Scientific and Industrial Research; Mr. S. K. Dutt, Science and Technology Specialist, American Embassy; Mr. R. C. Bhargava, Department of Power, Ministry of Energy; Mr. Vineet Nayyar, Ministry of Finance; Professor S. Chakravarty, Planning Commission and Chairman of Fuel Policy Committee; Mr. T. L. Sankar, Secretary to Fuel Policy Committee; Dr. K. S. Parikh, Director of Indian Statistical Institute and Member of Fuel Policy Committee; Dr. Deshpande, Department of Science and Technology; Mr. L. Kumar, Planning Commission. The author is grateful to each of these persons for sharing his time and knowledge.

number of reasons why hydropower development had not proceeded more rapidly.

One reason commonly given is that much of the hydro potential lies in areas with very rough terrain. Thirty percent of the total hydro potential lies in the Northeastern region which consists of the states of Assam, Maghalaya, Manipur, Nagaland, and Tripura, and the Union Territories of Arunachal Pradesh and Mizoram.[21] The potential hydropower sites are in mountainous areas with narrow valleys. The region is considered earthquake prone so construction standards are very strict. The large storage reservoirs require high dams, construction of which is quite difficult, time consuming, and costly. Virtually none of the enormous potential of this region has been developed.

Another reason development of hydropower in the Northeastern region has been delayed is lack of local demand. Previously, national or even large regional grids did not exist so power development was undertaken solely to satisfy demand in each state. With the development of a national grid and strong regional grids, this situation will change assuming interstate administrative problems can be overcome.

Interstate administrative problems constitute another major reason why hydropower development has been slow. As stated above, power development has been primarily the prerogative of the states. Hydropower projects often involve the participation of more than one state and the central government. This fact has caused countless administrative difficulties and delays in the formulation and implementation of multi-state hydropower projects.

Hydropower projects necessarily require long lead times from inception to power generation. The minimum lead time for most hydropower projects is eight years. Clearly, hydropower development does not fit conveniently into a five year planning period such as that used in India. The long lead times also cause problems when political pressures call for more immediate results. In fact, there was a shift in emphasis from hydropower to thermal power in the early 1970s caused primarily by the need for more immediate progress in power generation. One reason the shift was undertaken was because of the initial disappointment with progress in hydropower development. Too much was promised too soon, and the goals could not be achieved.

Another facet of the 'disappointment with hydropower' was that some felt hydropower was overly dependent on the weather. If the rains were good, hydropower was fine, but if the rains failed, hydropower did not live up to its potential. Hence, some policymakers felt hydropower was not dependable.

21. Central Electricity Authority, *Electric Power Survey*, p. 30.

The facts of the issue are quite to the contrary. According to J. P. Naegamvala, the performance of hydroelectric projects, '. . . has been generally above the designed level and in years of good water availability, they have contributed a good amount of secondary energy greatly mitigating power shortages in some of the systems.'[22] In other words, in bad years hydropower projects have generally produced only the prime power for which they were designed, but in good years they have produced extra power to alleviate shortages elsewhere in the power generation network. The actual 'disappointment' with hydropower has resulted from its inability to continue to take up the slack in the remainder of the system when weather conditions are unfavorable. Shortages have been so omnipresent that the power authorities came to depend upon secondary hydropower as part of the basic system. When this secondary power was not available, hydropower, rather than the overall shortage of generating capacity, received the blame for the ensuing outages. Hence, the reliability argument has little merit when correctly applied to a power generating system in which hydropower is only required to carry its slated portion of the load.

Another interesting reason for the lag in hydropower development is that hydropower is not on the frontier of science; consequently, it is of less interest to scientists. The technology is proven, and the remaining engineering problems are not particularly interesting to many scientists especially when compared with nuclear technology (fast breeder reactor or fusion) or the Magneto Hydro Dynamics (MHD) process of power generation.

One assessment of the hydropower development situation was that it is not correct to say that India did not develop hydropower for the reasons cited above. Rather, India developed hydropower at the rate and in the regions where it could be used at the time. Each hydropower investment had to be tailored to meet the needs of a particular demand area. Power development began with isolated demand areas and no national grid interconnecting these regions. Hence, there has been a time-phasing problem in hydropower development. It was not feasible to develop the rich Northeastern region until demand areas were more fully integrated and the power could be used to feed a national grid. Better transmission capability, and a set of interconnected regional grids, were required before the Northeastern hydropower potential could be productively utilized. Previously, these conditions were not met, and development of hydropower was (wisely) postponed. Now, however, the time

22. J. P. Naegamvala, 'Power Outlook in the Western Part of the Northern Region: A Case for Rapid Hydro-Electric Development,' *Indian Journal of Power and River Valley Development* (January 1975), pp. 1-14.

has come to develop this hydropower, as it can be productively utilized in the Indian power system.[23]

For the most part, this author concurs with this view of hydropower development in India. All of the reasons discussed above for the slow pace of hydropower development have some historical validity. And while they all point to legitimate problems in proceeding with hydropower development in years past, they also point to increasing the future pace of hydropower development. With rising world energy prices, the advantage of the renewable resource, hydropower, will be even greater. The Fifth and Sixth Plan allocations for the power sector should be increased substantially (see above) and hydropower development should receive a major share of this increased allocation.

Coal

This section provides a brief history of the organization of the coal industry, a discussion of the consumption patterns of coal in India, and a review of the relationship between coal production and power generation. The section concludes with a discussion of coal production projections, investment, and policy for the next decade.

Organization of the coal industry

Since pre-independence times coal mining in India was in the hands of the private sector.[24] In the early years, the technique of production known as 'slaughter' mining was sometimes employed. In this process, only the highest quality coal is mined and the remaining coal is lost for all time. Also, during this time, the working conditions in Indian coal fields were the subject of a great deal of concern. Although coal mining in any setting is a dangerous, dirty, arduous occupation, the working conditions in Indian coal fields were particularly bad.

Numerous committees were established through time to review mining techniques, mine safety, and the economic conditions of the coal industry. In 1936, an addendum to the *Coal Mining Committee Report* suggested that state ownership was the 'only ultimate solution' to the problems of the coal industry. The Mahindra committee of 1945 recommended a move towards state ownership of mineral rights and control of coal production. The government

23. The author is particularly grateful to Mr. R. C. Bhargava, Joint Secretary, Department of Power, Ministry of Energy, for sharing his insight on this issue.

24. The following discussion on the history of the organization of the coal industry in India is condensed from *Coal Industry in India* by S. Mohan Kumaramangalam, pp. 19-51.

did not move in this direction, however, and in 1955 the Coal Commissioner again advocated nationalizations saying, 'If nationalization is postponed by twenty-five years and the industry is given a free hand, there will be little left at the end of the period for the country to take over.'[25]

In 1955, a committee was established to study amalgamation of the numerous small inefficient coal fields. The committee recommended that mines producing less than ten thousand tons per month or mining less than one hundred acres be combined with adjacent mines. In 1958, a committee was created to encourage voluntary amalgamation, but over a period of fourteen years very little progress was made.

In May 1972, the coking coal mines in India were nationalized. This step was taken for the following reasons:

1. Government attempts to amalgamate the small inefficient mines had failed.
2. The reserves of coking coal are quite small in relation to the country's needs.
3. The mining techniques for coking coal resulted in a large amount of coal being wasted.
4. The mining process being followed in private sector mines was likely to cause serious damage to the mines and remaining coking coal reserves.

Coking coal mines were organized into the Bharat Coking Coal, Ltd., a public sector corporation.

In May 1973, all coal mines in India were nationalized. Kumaramangalam provides the following rationale for this step:

> The takeover of the non-coking coal mines was thus a response to the historical situation. Further inaction on the part of the Government would have meant permitting the continuance of unsound mining methods including slaughter mining, uneconomic collieries, mismanagement, unfair labour practices including underpayment of workers and malpractices in sales; and more than anything else it would have meant giving up the objective of establishment of a single authority, to whom the task of massive development in coal production as well as conservation and optimum utilization of our coal reserves could be entrusted.[26]

Public ownership of the coal industry was then split among three companies – Singareni Collieries (jointly owned by the Government of India and the state of Andhra Pradesh), Bharat Coking Coal, and the Coal Mines Authority.[27]

25. Kumaramangalam, p. 33.
26. Ibid., p. 50.
27. Henderson, p. 50.

In November 1975, these public sector organizations were combined into a single public sector corporation, Coal India Limited. This corporation now has the responsibility for all research, management, and production of coking and non-coking coal in India.[28]

Coal consumption in India

In 1974-75, 88.4 million tons of coal (excluding lignite) was produced in India. The Fuel Policy Committee estimated that 140.8 million tons per year would be required by the end of the Fifth Plan (1978-79) using end-use method number two described above. The composition of this projected consumption by final consumer group is shown in Table 33.

Table 33. Estimates of coal requirement for 1978-79.

Consuming sector	Coal requirement (million tons)
1. Steel plants and coke ovens	32
2. Thermal power generation	48
3. Transport (railways)	13
4. Industries	22
5. Brick burning	8
6. Domestic soft coke	10
7. Export	1
8. Consumption in coal mines	4
Total for energy use	138
Fertilizer feed stock	3
Total coal demand	141

Source: Government of India, *Report of the Fuel Policy Committee*, p. 18.

If the 48 million tons of coal required for thermal power generation is assumed to match the thermal (coal) portion of the 124 billion kilowatt hours of electrical energy required by the same forecasting technique, the coal required for the higher electrical energy forecasts can be calculated. Assuming coal based generation would be the same proportion of total power generated under each of the forecasts, the coal requirement for thermal generation would jump to 59.7 million tons if the energy requirement were 154.3 billion kilowatt hours (increase in the base forecast of 30 percent) and to 55.1 million tons if the energy requirement were 142.4 million kilowatt hours (20 percent

28. Personal communication with Mrs. Anjali Sen, Public Relations Officer, Coal India Limited, Calcutta, December 1975.

increase). Hence, increases in required power generation of 20 and 30 percent only mandate increases in total coal production of 5 to 8 percent respectively. Coal India Limited has been quite successfull in increasing coal production during its first year of operation, so this level of increase should be attainable.[29]

The Government of India, with assistance from the World Bank, is now undertaking a program to build some large (500 megawatt) thermal generating stations in India. Together with appropriate transmission and distribution facilities, this program should be of great help in increasing the level of installed capacity rapidly. Both the Government of India and the World Bank have realized the importance of the most economical placement of these large plants.[30] In the past with small generating plants, the plant site was normally adjacent to the demand area. However, for such large plants, a number of factors must be taken into account in determining proper plant placement including the following:

1. Expected costs of transporting coal to alternative sites.
2. Expected transmission losses from alternative sites to demand areas.
3. Constraints in transport of coal or power.
4. Growth patterns of power demand.
5. Existing size and mix of the power generation system.

The Fuel Policy Committee has recommended systems studies to evaluate these and other factors for future development of the power generation system. Indeed, an integrated view of the power generation system is a must if India is to provide adequately for the power requirements of the next decade.

Nuclear power

Only a small fraction of India's electric power is generated by nuclear power stations. In 1970-71 about 3 percent of the installed capacity was nuclear, and that proportion is expected to remain constant through 1978-79 with little change through the end of the Sixth Plan. However, a significant increase in nuclear power generation is slated by 1990-91.[31]

As indicated in Chapter 2, India has vast reserves of thorium, the feedstock for breeder reactors which are now in the development stage. It is hoped that

29. Personal communication with Mrs. Anjali Sen, Coal India Limited.
30. Personal conversations with Government of India and World Bank officials and *Report of the Fuel Policy Committee*, pp. 84-85.
31. G.o.I., *Fuel Policy Committee*, pp. 76-83.

the breeder reactor technology using thorium as a feedstock will be available by the early to mid 1980s, but this is not likely It is more likely that the breeder reactor will not be available for commercial applications until about 2000. Many planners and scientists in India indicated they felt this time horizon was realistic and felt that nuclear power could be counted on to make a substantial contribution in India only in the long term. Some officials believed that nuclear fusion was more like to be developed than the thorium based breeder reactor.[32] Fusion technology also is not expected to be ready for commerical application before the year 2000.

In summary, nuclear power is not now significant in India (nor in much of the rest of the world including the United States) and is not expected to become important for at least the next twenty years. There is, however, significant potential that nuclear energy could supply a larger portion of India's power needs beyond the year 2000.

RURAL ELECTRIFICATION

During the Fifth Plan rural electrification is included in the 'Minimum needs program' reflecting the importance attached to it by the Indian government.[33] The capital costs of rural electrification are quite high and a portion of the benefits are intangible or have a long gestation period. Benefits of rural electrification were described by the Fuel Policy Committee as follows:

> Electrification of a village not only adds to the productive capacities of the farmers but also brings with it social, civil and domestic amenities and has a salutary psychological effect on the rural people who start having a feel of the modern age.[34]

Some studies have shown that rural electrification has a positive benefit cost ratio, but it is generally conceded that rural electrification must involve an element of subsidy just as it has in the United States and in other countries.[35] In order to get the highest return from investment in rural electrification projects, the Fuel Policy Committee recommends a screening procedure to select those areas and villages where the returns will be highest. One major selection criterion is the potential increase in irrigated acreage which could result from the availability of electricity for pump sets. In recent years the Government has shifted its focus somewhat and is reporting figures on pump sets energized as well as villages electrified. During the Fifth Plan, the goal is

32. From interviews and discussions with the G.o.I. officials listed above.
33. G.o.I., *Draft: Fifth Plan*, 2: 125.
34. G.o.I., *Fuel Policy Committee*, p. 85.
35. Venkataraman, pp. 94-99.

to energize 1.5 million pump sets and to electrify 110, 000 villages.[36] Progress in rural electrification from 1961 to 1970 is shown in Table 34.

Table 34. Progress in rural electrification in India.

Village population (1961 census)	Total	No. elect. in 1961	Percent of total	No. elect. in 1970	Percent of total
1-499	351,653	3,986	1	26,222	7
500-999	119,086	4,306	4	21,775	18
1000-1999	65,377	5,918	9	22,504	34
2000-4999	26,565	5,458	21	15,948	60
5000-9999	3,421	1,319	39	2,638	77
10,000+	776	560	72	693	89
Totals	566,878	21,547	4	89,780	16

Source: Government of India, *Report of the Fuel Policy Committee*, p. 86.

As can be seen from Table 34, significant progress has been made, especially in the larger village categories. However, as of 1970, only 10 percent of the villages of less than one thousand population had been electrified. It is these villages, many of which are more remote, that are expensive to electrify and which produce the lowest economic benefits. Chapter 6 evaluates the potential of decentralized rural electrification using biogas versus the cost of centralized thermal based power generation.

SUMMARY

The major conclusions of this chapter may be summarized rather succinctly. First, the forecasting procedures currently being used in India result in forecasts which understate the actual future demand because they are based on periods when supply was constrained. To relieve power shortages and assure an adequate reserve supply, the installed generating capacity needs to be increased at a much greater rate than planned.

Second, development of hydroelectric potential in India has proceeded rather slowly. There are a number of good reasons why hydropower development has lagged in the past. Now that strong regional grids and a national grid are a reality, however, hydropower development should proceed at a

36. G.o.I., *Draft: Fifth Plan*, 2: 125.

rapid pace. Hydropower can now be generated in the Northeastern region where it is so abundant, and the power utilized in other parts of the country. Some administrative changes in state control over power development would be useful in facilitating this effort.

Third, India's non-coking coal reserves will last for many years. In order to increase power generation to an adequate level in the near term, coal production will have to increase significantly. With the recent success of Coal India, Ltd. in achieving higher production levels, this increase should be feasible.

Fourth, nuclear power is not an important part of the power picture in India for at least the next decade and probably for the next quarter century. Although India is richly endowed with thorium, it will not play an important part in the energy economy until at least the turn of the century.

Fifth, one means of 'bringing village India into the modern age' is rural electrification. Although the cost of rural electrification is very high, it probably achieves social benefits at least equal to its costs. The progress of rural electrification to date with centralized power generation was examined in this chapter; alternative means of rural electrification will be evaluated in the next chapter.

6. Biogas and other alternative energy sources

Of the possible alternative energy sources mentioned in Chapter 2, only biogas and solar energy offer significant potential for use in India during the next quarter century. This chapter evaluates the potential for using biogas as an alternative means of rural electrification (through decentralized power generation) and as a means of providing both fuel for direct consumption and fertilizer to village India. The potential for solar energy development in India is also reviewed.

BIOGAS BASED POWER GENERATION

One possible means of providing electricity to India's 550,000 villages is by using animal, human, and possibly some forms of vegetable waste to make methane, a fuel that can be employed in small generators located in or near the communities to be served. This method is often called the gobar gas process in India since 'gobar' – cattle dung – is the main ingredient. The principal alternative, and the one that has been pushed in recent drives for rural electrification, is large-scale power works, using coal, hydroelectric potential, atomic energy, or now possibly oil or gas. Reliance upon the large-scale system mandates an extensive power grid, which the local system does not. The Indian government is considering a commitment to a sizeable small.scale power program, possibly assisted by multilateral foreign aid. The economic basis of this decision and its ramifications for rural society have not, however, been systematically assessed.

In this chapter a cost analysis of the two major rural power options is undertaken: central power facilities and biogas units. The findings are contrasted with the estimates of the major previous studies of biogas electrification. In the author's judgment, previous cost estimates have been substantially biased towards local units. The conclusion reached by this author is that, on average, centralized power production and distribution have an appreciable cost advantage over local units. Where villages are remote from transmission lines, however, small scale units may provide a cost savings. There are thus numerous locations in rural India where gobar gas facilities may serve at least as a transitional source of power. In those instances, the administrative problems associated with providing and servicing these decentralized generators and the implications of implanting this new technology in the Indian village setting are a source of concern.

That biological materials can be used to generate combustible gases has been known for some time. In northern Italy in 1776, Alessandra Volta recognized the correspondence between the volume of combustible gas generated by lake sediments and the amount of plant material in the sediment. During the Second World War a number of vehicles in Germany were converted to methane operation. Research in India began at the Indian Agricultural Research Institute in 1939. Although a number of experimental plants were developed, it was not until the early 1960s that a practical design was available for field use.

The principal energy ingredient in biogas is methane, CH_4, or natural gas. Biogas is formed in one of two ways: (1) When organic material is left exposed to the air, the gaseous byproducts of decay escape into the atmosphere, and the residue is compost. This decay process is termed aerobic because it is enabled by bacteria that work in the presence of oxygen. (2) The process of forming useful biogas is known as anaerobic digestion since it occurs in the absence of oxygen. During the first phase, sludge materials are broken down into smaller molecules. Organic compounds are oxidized to acids or alcohols, the oxygen in the material fed to the digestor is used up, and large amounts of carbon dioxide are formed. In the second phase, bacteria convert the acids and alcohols into methane and carbon dioxide. Generally, 60 to 70 percent of the gas formed is methane. A delicately balanced environment is required. Changes in acidity, temperature, input mix, and other factors affect the pace and yield of the reactions. For example, the amount of gas generated is a function of temperature. About twice the amount of gas per ton of manure is produced at 75° C (167° F) as at 25° C (77° F). Methane generation stops completely below 10° C (50° F). Temperatures in North India in the winter frequently fall beneath this threshold and under such conditions some biogas may have to be used to provide heat for the plant, thereby reducing its net yield.

Cost of centralized power generation

In order to calculate an estimated cost of electricity per kilowatt hour, it is necessary first to estimate the initial capital costs. Capital costs of either biogas or central power facilities include three components: the cost of the power plant, transmission costs, and the cost of village electrification. The ultimate calculation of capital costs per kilowatt hour depends not only upon these cost estimates but upon utilization factors – that is, the degree to which installed capacity is utilized. Unreasonable assumptions regarding any of the capital cost components or the utilization factors will substantially bias the final cost per kilowatt hour estimate.

A number of studies have attempted to compute the costs of installing and operating gobar gas units. Among these, only a few have compared rural electrification using biogas with centralized generation alternatives.[1] Makhijani and Poole estimated the total capital cost for coal-fired generating plants in India at $500 per kilowatt. This cost estimate included $250 per kilowatt for the generating station, $50 per kilowatt for transmission, and $200 per kilowatt for rural electrification. Capital cost for thermal generating plants in 1970 was about $200 per kilowatt.[2] The generation station and transmission costs reported by Makhijani and Poole for 1974 appear somewhat high but reasonable, allowing for inflation. At a 12 percent discount rate the annual amortization per kilowatt is $60.[3]

Their rural distribution cost estimate assumes that the average transmission distance from the main line to each village is eight kilometers. Joint distribution to several villages would reduce these costs. It is clear, too, that costs for a given village will be lower the nearer it is situated to major power lines and that with the growth of India's national power system more and more villages will be closer to such lines. Without knowing the exact distribution costs for a particular village, it is impossible to determine whether central or biogas costs per kilowatt hour would be lower. Estimates that use average distribution costs can thus only provide a basis for a general comparison of the two systems.

1. See Arjun Makhijani and Alan Poole, *Energy and Agriculture in the Third World* (Cambridge: Ballinger Publishing Co., 1975); C. R. Prasad, K. Krishna Prasad, and A. K. N. Reddy, 'Biogas Plants: Prospects, Problems, and Tasks,' *Economic and Political Weekly*, Special Number, August 1974, pp. 1347-1364; M. A. Sathianathan, *Biogas: Achievement and Challenges* (New Delhi: Association of Voluntary Agencies for Rural Development, 1975); a more general survey is found in Roger Revelle, 'Energy Use in Rural India,' *Science* 192 (4 June 1976), pp. 969-975.
2. G.o.I., *Fuel Policy Committee*, p. 84.
3. Makhijani and Poole used a 15 percent discount rate, but to achieve consistency with their analysis of a typical decentralized unit it is necessary to use a 12 percent rate.

To convert the annual capital charge of $60 per kilowatt to cost per kilowatt hour, utilization factors must be employed. For centralized power generation, a proper approach is to separate rural distribution costs from generation and transmission costs and apply an appropriate utilization factor to each portion. The average generating plant utilization factor for India as a whole has been in the range of 48 to 55 percent, which is comparable to the average plant utilization factor for the United States.[4] The plant utilization factor should be applied to the generation and transmission portion of total capital cost ($300 or $36 per year at a 12 percent discount rate). The appropriate factor for rural distribution cost ($200 or $24 per year at a 12 percent discount rate) is derived from the rate of power consumption per kilowatt of connected load in rural areas. From 1966 to 1971, agricultural sector consumption in India ranged from 657 to 842 kilowatt hours per kilowatt of connected load representing distribution network utilization of 8 to 10 percent.[5] Total rural sector consumption rates would be somewhat higher.

In their analysis, Makhijani and Poole used the same utilization factor for both generation and transmission and rural distribution. They used two different factors: 1150 and 800 kilowatt hours per kilowatt per year which represent 13 and 10 percent utilization factors respectively.[6] These factors are appropriate for the rural distribution component but not for the generation and transmission components of total capital cost. Makhijani and Poole evidently believe that a power plant would serve only rural areas, that no urban or industrial consumption would be serviced from the plant.

Table 35 displays a range of unit costs of centralized power supply; it includes my estimates as well as those of Makhijani and Poole and others. Items one and two are actual unit cost calculations by Henderson (2.2 cents per kilowatt hour) and Venkataraman (1.5 cents). The two Makhijani and Poole estimates for their assumed 10 percent and 13 percent capacity utilization factors are 8.5 cents and 6.2 cents per kilowatt hour, respectively. Item five is the author's estimate. A plant utilization factor of 45 percent is assumed which yields a capital amortization cost for generation and transmission of .9 cents per kilowatt hour. Assuming rural consumption of 1100 kilowatt hours per kilowatt of connected load (12.6 percent utilization), capital amortization cost for rural distribution becomes 2.2 cents per kilowatt hour. Hence, the total value for amortized capital cost is 3.1 cents per kilowatt hour (using a 12

4. *Statistical Yearbook of the Electrical Utility Industry for 1974* (New York: Edison Electric Institute, 1975), pp. 6-15; G.o.I., *Fuel Policy Committee*, p. 80.
5. G.o.I., *Fuel Policy Committee*, p. 87.
6. Makhijani and Poole, p. 97.

percent discount rate). If Henderson's operating cost per kilowatt hour of 1.3 cents is raised to 1.5 cents to allow for inflation, the total unit cost of centralized fossil fuel power generation for rural areas becomes 4.6 cents per kilowatt hour. Because this cost estimate was calculated using conservative utilization factors, it should be considered the upper limit for centralized power costs for villages an 'average' distance from power lines. This cost estimate will be compared with the biogas generation cost estimates discussed below.

Table 35. Unit cost of centralized electricity supply in India.

	Capital cost-amortization (cents per kwh)	Operating cost (cents per kwh)	Total unit cost (cents per kwh)
1. actual 1971-1972 costs	.9	1.3	2.2
2. actual 1967-1968 costs	.8	.7	1.5
3. capacity utilization = 10 percent 800 kwh/kw/yr	7.5	1.0	8.5
4. capacity utilization = 13 percent 1150 kwh/kw/yr	5.2	1.0	6.2
5. plant capacity utilization = 45 percent rural distribution utilization = 13 percent 3942 and 1100 kwh/kw/yr	3.1	1.5	4.6

Sources: (1) Henderson, p. 87; (2) Venkataraman, pp. 84-88; (3) and (4) Makhijani and Poole, pp. 97-98; (5) author's calculations.

Biogas based power generation

The physical parameters controlling the generation of electricity using a decentralized biogas system are summarized in Table 36. Column one contains the author's estimates; columns two and three show comparable data from other sources. In an average village there are in the neighborhood of 250 to 300 cattle. Assuming that each animal will provide about three kilograms of dry dung each day and that three-quarters of that amount is collected for use, the total amount available will be 675 kilograms. This estimate is thus higher than those of Prasad *et al.* (596 kilograms) and of Makhijani and Poole (622 kilograms). Multiplication of usable dry dung by the biogas yield per kilogram (eleven cubic feet) and by the BTU content of a cubic foot of gas, yields the total BTU content. When this total is divided by the energy conversion factor and multiplied by the efficiency of the power generator, a maximum power generation estimate is derived. This is 337 kilowatt hours per day, and is lower than those calculated by Prasad *et al.* and Makhijani-Poole. Nonetheless, this is an optimistic value and an upper limit with current technology.

The differences among the three results are due to the use of different yield and conversion estimates. Makhijani and Poole assumed a 60 percent conversion efficiency which is near the highest observed in experimental plants.[7] Prasad, *et al.* assumed a conversion efficiency of only 30 percent and this is slightly below the year round average for India. It appears that 50 percent net energy conversion generally may be attainable after additional applied research and development. This figure, which is comparable to 11 cubic feet of biogas per kilogram of dry dung was used for the author's calculations. The next key assumption concerns power generation efficiency; that is, the efficiency of the internal combustion engine and generator in converting biogas energy into electric power. Makhijani and Poole assume a generation efficiency of 25 percent which is probably near the upper limit.[8] Although gasoline engines usually run at less than 25 percent efficiency, this level was selected to represent the best possible case. Based on these assumptions, the maximum power that could be generated per day is 337 kilowatt hours.

The costs of generating power may be estimated on two different bases: (1) assuming a portion of the biogas is used for cooking to replace dung that was previously used for this purpose; and (2) assuming a substitute (perhaps solar energy or water hyacinths) could be found for cooking so that all biogas could be used to generate electricity. The adjusted initial capital and annual costs of these two alternatives are given in Table 37. Following Makhijani and Poole, 46 percent of the biogas generated is assumed to be adequate to serve the cooking needs of two hundred families in the village. This fraction may be low in light of the technical difficulties in maintaining a high level of production. Nonetheless, the analysis of capital costs is based on this assumption. For the applications with and without biogas used for cooking, it is asserted that the costs of the biogasification plant, the gas plant auxiliaries, land, and gas storage and compression would be identical. This procedure is valid for the first three items but is open to question for gas storage and compression. Storage facilities adequate for 50 percent of the annual production of gas were

7. Makhijani and Poole, p. 149; also see, Sathianathan, pp. 31-34; Prasad *et al.*, pp. 134-39.
8. Sathianathan, pp. 68-69.

Table 36. Assumptions used for biogas power generation.

Item	Units	Author's values	Prasad, Prasad, and Reddy	Makhijani and Poole
1. Dry dung/cow/day	kg.	3.0	3.18	2.96
2. No. of cattle in village		300	250	300
3. Dry dung/village/day	kg.	900	795	888
4. Collection efficiency	%	75	75	70
5. Usable dry dung/village/day	kg.	675	596	622
6. Biogas yield/kg. dry dung	cu.ft.	11	6.6	13.5[a]
7. Energy content/cu.ft. of biogas[b]	BTU	620	620	620
8. Conversion factor	kwh/BTU	3413	3413	3413
9. Power generating efficiency	%	25	83[c]	25
10. Maximum power generation/day	kwh	337	593	381

[a]Biogas yield for the Makhijani and Poole study was calculated by multiplying the energy content of dry dung (14,000 BTU/kg.) by the assumed conversion efficiency of 60 percent, and dividing the result by 620 BTU/cu.ft. This yield is equivalent to 6 cu.ft./1b. of dry dung which is the expected biogas yield at 27°C (80°F). Clearly, a net yield of this magnitude is not currently attainable during winter months in North India.

[b]Sathianathan, p. 62.

[c]Prasad, Prasad, and Reddy make the direct conversion from cubic feet of biogas to kwh using a factor of .15 kwh/cu.ft. biogas. Assuming 620 BTU/cu.ft. of biogas, this conversion amounts to a generation efficiency of 83 percent.

Table 37. Costs of a decentralized biogas generation and electrification plant.

Cost item	Gas used for cooking[a]	Alternative cooking fuel[a]
	Capital costs	
Biogasification plant	$ 8,000	$ 8,000
Gas plant auxiliaries	1,000	1,000
Land cost	1,000	1,000
Gas storage and compression	1,000	1,500
Cooking fuel distribution cylinders and gas stoves	8,000	——
Cost of water hyacinth or other cooking system	——	10,000
Electric generator with reciprocating gas engine and switchgear at 160/kw installed	10,600	19,700
Construction supervision and training	1,000	1,000
Subtotal	$ 30,600	$ 42,200
Interest on capital during six months' construction at 12 percent	1,800	2,500
Total	$ 32,400	$ 44,700
Cost per kilowatt	491	363
	Annual costs	
Capital cost amortization	$ 4,100	$ 5,700
Residue collection at $2/ton fresh manure	2,600	2,600
Local labor and maintenance	1,300	1,300
Market town services	500	500
Labor for distributing cooking fuel	300	600
Gross annual costs	$ 8,800	$10,700
Credit for cooking fuel sales	2,000	2,000
Credit for fertilizer	2,400	2,400
Total credits	$ 4,400	$ 4,400
Net annual operating cost	4,400	6,300
Annual electricity generation at 1,000 kwh/kw	66,000 kwh	123,000 kwh
Cost per kilowatt	6.7c	5.1c

Source: These cost estimates are adapted from cost values contained in Makhijani and Poole, pp. 112-116.

[a]All costs are rounded to the nearest $100.

assumed in both cases. This assumption is reasonable for the case without cooking fuel but appears to be too high for the case with cooking fuel because daily utilization of gas for cooking would even out the consumption pattern through time relative to the case without cooking fuel. Hence, the storage and compression cost for the case with cooking fuel was reduced to account for this difference.

Table 37 displays the revised capital and annual costs for the two cases assuming generator capacities of 66 kilowatts and 123 kilowatts. Makhijani and Poole used generator sizes of 75 kilowatts and 140 kilowatts for the with and without cooking cases respectively. Because a lower maximum daily generation figure was used for the author's calculations, the generation capacities and cost figures were also recalculated. Makhijani and Poole assumed no economies of scale for the higher capacity generators, an hypothesis retained by the author.

Gross annual cost for a biogas plant is calculated by amortizing at a 12 percent discount rate the total initial plant investment and adding four additional costs: collection costs, labor and maintenance, market town services, and distribution costs of fuel. A twenty-five year life is assumed for the biogas plant and other equipment, which may be somewhat long given the corrosive nature of some of the materials used in biogas generation.

After figuring gross annual operating costs, it is necessary to subtract credits for cooking fuel sales and a credit for fertilizer sales to obtain a figure for net annual operating costs. Annual electricity generation was figured on the basis of 1000 kilowatt hours per kilowatt installed, the figure used by Makhijani and Poole, which represents a capacity figure of 11.4 percent.[9] Since all of the electricity generated from the biogas plant would be used in a limited rural area, this capacity utilization represents an upper limit. Using the above assumptions and cost input data, the cost per kilowatt hour of electricity with biogas used for cooking would be 6.7 cents and with no cooking provided from the biogas, 5.1 cents. Since assumptions favorable to biogas generation were used when no firm data were available, these costs represent lower limits of the costs for biogas based generation.

Comparison of cost estimates

Clearly, both of the biogas cost estimates are greater than the 4.6 cents per kilowatt hour cost for the centralized power generation system. It should be

9. This capacity fraction is somewhat lower than that used for the centralized system because greater capacity is required in the decentralized system for the same load due to the heavy demand of motor starting requirements (Makhijani and Poole, p. 116).

emphasized that 4.6 cents per kilowatt hour represents the upper limit for the 'average' village and that 5.1 cents per kilowatt hour represents the lower limit for power generation using the biogas system. Actual differences may be considerably greater. Based on economic considerations alone, the conclusion of this analysis is that *electricity generation using centralized power facilities is on average more cost advantageous than adopting decentralized systems based on biogas generation.*[10]

In some situations, however, power generation from gobar gas may be a reasonable alternative. In isolated regions, the transmission costs would be higher than those estimated. Small villages, or even caste or lineage neighborhoods, might use biogas as an interim alternative to a central source. Even if only 20 percent of India's villages fall into these categories, over 100,000 units would be installed.

It should be noted that the conclusion applies only to the use of biogas as a means of decentralized electric power generation. The merits of gobar gas as a cleaner more healthful cooking fuel, and the potential of the residue being a superior fertilizer have not been considered. A biogas program may be desirable solely as a means of producing both cooking fuel and fertilizer from cow dung with no associated power generation.

BIOGAS FUEL GENERATION

The major problem with biogas based power generation lies in the transformation of the biogas energy into electrical energy. Small scale generators are not efficient converters of energy and even the expensive process of rural electrification appears to be a preferred option. However, use of the biogas energy directly as fuel is more attractive. Biogas could be used both for heat and light, and perhaps for other purposes such as pump sets. Kirit Parikh has demonstrated that biogas plants are both profitable from a private point of view and beneficial from a social viewpoint.[11]

Table 38 provides the yield assumptions used by Parikh in his biogas analysis. He assumes the private owner has five cattle which produce an average of 2.7 kilograms of dry dung per day. With a 75 percent collection efficiency, the available dry dung per day is ten kilograms. Parikh assumes a biogas yield of 6.4 cubic feet per kilogram of dry dung and a gas energy content of 535

10. Venkataraman reports that average cost of electrifying a village in India is about $9000, much less than the cost of a biogas electrification unit (p. 94). K. Venkataraman, *Power Development in India, The Financial Aspects* (New Delhi: Wiley Eastern Pvt. Ltd., 1972).
11. Parikh, *Energy*, pp. 93-106.

British Thermal Units. Multiplying the daily yield of usable dry dung by the biogas yield and by the energy content yields 34,200 British Thermal Units of energy per day. With a burning efficiency of 60 percent, 20,500 British Thermal Units of energy would be available.

Table 38. Fuel energy available from private biogas units.

Item	Units	Values
1. Dry dung/cow/day	kg.	2.7
2. Cattle/family		5
3. Dry dung/family/day	kg.	13.5
4. Collection efficiency	%	75
5. Usable dry dung/family/day	kg.	10.0
6. Biogas yield/kg. dry dung	cu.ft.	6.4
7. Energy content/cu.ft. of biogas	BTU	535
8. Burning efficiency	%	60
9. Usable fuel energy/day	BTU	20,500

Source: Kirit Parikh, *Energy*, pp. 95-98.

By comparing Tables 36 and 38, it can be seen that the assumptions used for these calculations are in every instance equal to or more conservative than the assumptions used in the analysis for power generation potential.

Even with this conservative set of assumptions, the energy yield from the biogas is greater than the energy yield obtained from directly burning the dung. The energy content of dried dung is about 14,000 BTU/kilogram. Burning efficiency of cow dung cakes is much lower than biogas burning efficiency. Parikh estimates this efficiency at 11 percent which yields 15,400 British Thermal Units per day, 25 percent less than the biogas system. In addition, the fertilizer value is lost when the dung is burned. Parikh calculates a private rate of return for biogas units of 14 to 18 percent.[12]

A major drawback to private units such as the one described above is that they would benefit only rich cattle owners. For this reason, the government of India is considering a program for village sized biogas units. The larger units achieve economies of scale which means that, economically, they are even more attractive.[13] With the biogas used for both heat (cooking and some space heat) and light, significant energy savings in other sources would be achieved. Parikh estimated that with a heavy emphasis on biogas installations, four million tons of kerosene could be saved annually. This amount is

12. Ibid., pp. 93-98.
13. Ibid., pp. 103-4; and Sathianathan, pp. 162-67.

equivalent to 4.2 million tons of diesel which would be adequate for providing energy to 21 million pump sets each year.[14] All the problems with biogas production have not been solved, but biogas production for direct fuel use appears to have considerable potential.

POTENTIAL PROBLEMS WITH A BIOGAS GENERATION PROGRAM

Before biogas is adopted in those circumstances where it is deemed desirable, there are a number of political and administrative problems that need to be resolved at the national level. In addition, if past experience with agricultural assistance, community development, and cooperative credit institutions at the village level is any guide, the villagers of India are likely to find their lives deeply affected by the program; and, in turn, they are likely to bend biogas installations to their own purposes and thereby upend the calculations of policy-makers who ignore the human factor.

The general administrative problems likely to be encountered are those typical of any new program. These include coordination of finance, production, distribution, and political activities together with assuring adequate numbers and competence of staff to carry forward the assigned tasks. Any massive diffusion of technology depends upon the dissemination of information, guidance of production and distribution by cooperation between technicians and the service population, and adequate provision for maintenance. A successful biogas program must be based on a technically sound plant which can function under a wide range of operating conditions. Much research needs to be done on plant design for improved efficiency, improved winter operating performance, use of solar energy to heat the biogas plant, proper utilization of the sludge output to conserve nutrients, and biogas plant operations in water short regions. Initial breakdowns in administration, maintenance, or technical components may sour villagers on the program, and they and their neighbors may become progressively unresponsive.

There is also the danger that new biogas units will be emplaced in villages which are close to existing roads, towns, and power lines. This pattern may tend to result from ease of access for construction, maintenance, and monitoring. Yet these are the sites where biogas power generation offers little or no cost advantage and where commercial energy is more readily available. Officials will have to take special steps to ensure that decentralized rural electrification or biogas fuel generation reaches into the more remote areas

14. Parikh, *Energy*, p. 106.

where it will do the most good and does not end up as merely another facility provided to the already built-up regions.

Major obstacles to the successful dissemination and utilization of biogas plants in Indian villages are found at the village level. Currently, cow dung is used directly for fuel and compost in many Indian villages, and there is an existing social-cum-economic structure that provides for the collection, drying, and distribution of the dung fuel. The institutional structure is so arranged that, generally, fuel is available for the cooking needs of villagers in all castes or economic classes, and without regard to the distribution of cattle ownership.

If a biogas plant is established, then cow dung would not be used directly as a fuel but would be 'transformed' into another type of fuel and fertilizer. One could anticipate that many of the types of tensions associated with commercialization of the village economic system and with the adoption of new farm technologies would recur. As in these previous cases, the new development provides novel opportunities for gain for some villagers and threatens to deprive others of existing income rights. In turn, these economic changes will interact with caste and status relationships and with the village political system. At present, dung is a nonmarketed commodity subject to rules and rights that govern its sharing. As with crops, labor, land, and water, dung will become a marketed and priced item subject to distribution through the market system. It is reasonable to suppose that the village cattle owners, who are likely in the main to be the wealthier peasant farmers, will attempt to assert latent property rights to their beasts' dung. Their power and status are likely to enable them to get their way. The losers will be the poorer families whose women and children collect dung for cooking. They will have to seek alternative sources of fuel. Some may even lose small incomes from the sale of dried dung.

On the distribution side, some equitable and enforceable method must be devised for governing the flow of gas or electricity and fertilizer. Even if initial efforts to ensure even-handed community control and to design an equitable pattern are successful (which is not likely), it would be surprising if the big men of the village were not able to abort these, place themselves astride power and gas lines, and appropriate more than their share of energy and fertilizer.

One may with some confidence predict a worsening of the internal distribution of resources and incomes inside the village. A prerequisite to taking the biogas system into village India must be the design of a set of locally intelligible property rights and payments that do not do excessive violence to existing economic relationships – it is too much to expect a change for the better. At a minimum, some serious thought must be given to determining what effects the new technology will have on village institutions and how the villagers will respond.

SOLAR ENERGY

Solar energy is believed to offer significant potential as a future source of energy for India. The Science and Technology Plan recommended investing 25 million rupees in solar energy development during the Fifth Plan.[15] Several different solar energy projects will be undertaken during this time.

One area of emphasis is in developing a solar powered water pump. Two different techniques are being explored to develop solar pumps suitable for irrigation. Both involve employing solar collectors to heat water which in turn is used to evaporate an organic liquid. The vaporized liquid generates pressure which is utilized in pumping water.[16] If solar powered pumps are perfected, they could be very beneficial in spreading the benefits of irrigation without utilizing non-renewable energy resources.

The Motilal Nehru Engineering College at Allahabad in cooperation with other institutions is trying to develop solar collectors which use parabolic reflectors to concentrate solar energy to produce steam to run mechanical devices. In addition, work is progressing to produce a silicon solar cell capable of producing fifty to one hundred watts of electricity.

Annamalai University has developed a solar powered paddy drier with a capacity of two hundred kilograms per day and is working on a drier with a one ton per day capacity. A solar powered kiln for seasoning wood has been developed by the Forest Research Institute at Dehra Dun. Other solar energy projects with agricultural applications are being developed at various research institutions within India.

In addition, foreign scientists from Australia and West Germany are collaborating with Indian scientists to develop small scale solar power plants, solar water heaters, and other solar energy devices.[17] Both scientists and government officials in India see great promise for solar energy development in the next quarter century. Most of the solar energy projects are still in the research and development stage, but it appears likely that economically viable products and processes will be available within five to ten years.

15. National Committee on Science and Technology (Government of India), *Draft Science and Technology Plan 1974-79* (Delhi: INSDOC, 1973) 2: 151.
16. Interview with Mr. S. K. Dutt, Science and Technology Specialist, American Embassy, New Delhi, India, December 1975.
17. Ibid.

7. Conclusions and policy recommendations

In the first three chapters of this study, the relationship between energy consumption and national income was described, the potential energy resources available to India were evaluated, and the past history of energy resource development in the five year plans was reviewed. In Chapters 4, 5, and 6, we analyzed current and potential future energy supply policies for oil and natural gas, power (including hydropower, coal, and nuclear based generation), and biogas and solar energy sources. In this chapter we bring together the results of this research to provide a comprehensive review of energy supply policy in India. Conclusions from the chapters on individual energy sectors are first summarized and then integrated to illuminate the relationships among energy sectors. Environmental effects of energy resource development in India are briefly reviewed. Finally, policy alternatives for energy resource development in India are examined.

OIL AND NATURAL GAS

Until recently, very little exploration and development of India's petroleum resources had taken place. In 1974, however, India discovered a large field at Bombay High and has since made another significant discovery. India's prospects for reducing her dependence on foreign oil are quite bright. However, exploring for and developing oil resources is a highly capital intensive operation. India quadrupled the original Fifth Plan budget for the oil sector primarily to finance further exploration and development work in or near the recent discoveries. This investment requires mostly foreign exchange because oil exploration and development (particularly offshore) requires the use of advanced foreign technology.

An alternative to financing all the needed exploration and development is for India to lease portions of its offshore areas to foreign firms. India has already issued three leases to American and Canadian firms and has the opportunity of issuing additional leases in the future.

The leasing system used in India is known as a production sharing contract. In return for financing all exploration and development expenditures, the lessee is given a portion of the oil which is produced from the lease. If no oil is found, the contract is cancelled and the lessee provides the Government of India with all data produced from the lease area. If oil is found, it is shared according to a complex set of arrangements allowing for recovery of original cost plus a return to capital.

The economic relationships of the Indian leasing system were modeled in a comprehensive resource policy evaluation model. In addition, features of leasing systems in use or proposed for use in the United States, Great Britain, and Peru were incorporated in the model. The Indian leasing system was compared with those being used (or proposed) for other countries, and was found to function quite well in capturing a large share of the economic rent for the Government of India. The Indian system was clearly superior to that being used in Peru and under most assumptions superior to the present United States' system. Performance of the Indian system was marginally inferior to capital recovery systems proposed for future use in the United States and other countries. It appears that India could lease substantial amounts of offshore area, achieve rapid exploration and development of her petroleum resources, and lose a relatively small proportion of the oil produced. At the same time, India would not have to finance the huge initial outlays for exploration and development.

POWER DEVELOPMENT

During the first four plans, progress in power development consistently fell behind schedule. During the Fourth Plan, the shortfall amounted to 50 percent of planned development. These shortfalls have led to critical power shortages in India which have constrained both agricultural and industrial growth.

The current procedure for planning future power generating requirements tends to perpetuate these shortages. Power requirements are projected based on power consumption during past years. However, power consumption in the past was sometimes severely constrained. The 'true' level of power demand for this period is not known, but it is certain to be higher than the (constrained) level of actual consumption. Hence, the unconstrained demand for future periods would be higher.

In addition, the actual demand for electric power would have been greater if adequate power supplies were assured. Assured availability of power would stimulate investment in power consumptive industries (and agriculture) and power generating capacity requirements would be increased. Projected power generating capacity requirements should be increased substantially to avoid perpetuating power shortages.

Hydropower

With at least 41 million kilowatts of hydropower potential, India ranks seventh among world countries in hydropower resources. At this time, however, only about 18 percent of this resource has been developed or is under development. There are several good reasons why hydropower development has proceeded at a slow pace in the past. Much of the hydropower potential is located at a distance from demand areas. Previously, there was no national electric grid so power was not easily shifted from one area to another. Power development proceeded by supplying individual demand areas until the transmission infrastructure was sufficiently developed to integrate local or regional grids. Now that regional grids are a reality, hydropower development in locations distant from major demand areas can be undertaken.

Other reasons for the lag in hydropower development relate to the long lead times and difficulty of construction. Hydropower installations are required in locations with rugged terrain. Some of the regions are earthquake prone, so construction standards are quite rigid. Because it normally takes at least eight years to complete a major hydropower project, careful planning is required. In the early 1970s when the power situation became critical, the long lead times caused a shift in emphasis towards coal based generation with its shorter lead times.

Hydropower also has been criticized for being overly dependent on the weather and incapable of meeting generating requirements when rains are below normal. Undoubtedly, hydropower is to some extent dependent on the weather. However, the situation in India is that hydropower was generating more power than designed, and with the slow pace of building generating capacity, power officials came to depend on the additional hydropower. Consequently, when the rains were poor and the power situation worsened, hydropower received the blame. The real cause, of course, was the slow rate of growth of power generation capacity.

Hydropower is a renewable resource with which India is richly endowed. In the future, hydropower should receive greater emphasis as India increases its power generation capacity.

Coal

India is adequately endowed with non-coking coal to last at least eighty years. However, coking coal reserves are a problem and are expected to last only about forty years. After a long history of public sector displeasure over private sector performance, all coal mines in India were nationalized in 1973. In 1975, a single public sector corporation, Coal India Limited, was established to manage and produce India's coal resources.

Although the Fuel Policy Committee estimated coal requirements in 1978-79 of 141 million tons, the Fifth Plan calls for increasing production to only 135 million tons. Two items could account for this discrepancy. First, consumption in coal mines (4 million tons) is excluded from the Plan estimate. Second, the Fuel Policy Committee included 3 million tons for fertilizer feed stock. With the large natural gas discoveries at Bombay High and Bassein, it is more likely that this resource, will be used for fertilizer production. Given recent progress in coal production, it appears likely that the coal production target can be achieved. However, if the power generation capacity is increased beyond the level stipulated in the Fifth Plan, more coal would have to be produced than planned. Even if power generation capacity is increased 20 to 30 percent, only a 5 to 8 percent increase in total coal production (beyond the planned level) would be required. With additional investments in coal production, this increase should be attainable.

Nuclear

Only about 3 percent of India's electric power is generated from nuclear sources. This percentage is not expected to change markedly for at least fifteen years. India is not richly endowed with uranium resources, so any massive investment in nuclear power would make India dependent on foreign supplies of fuel, a situation she is trying to avoid.

For the long term, India is richly endowed with thorium, a feedstock for the breeder reactor. During the Fifth and Sixth Plans, India plans to build and utilize a prototype 40 megawatt fast breeder reactor. If the breeder reactor does become commercially feasible, and other obstacles are overcome (social resistance, safety, proliferation), India would be in a very good position with respect to power generation. India's thorium reserves could last almost indefinitely. However, at this time, the thorium based breeder reactor is still in the research and development stage.

Alternative rate structures

In India, the United States, and other countries, energy conservation is being viewed as a means of alleviating energy shortages. One means of conserving electric energy is by modifying the rate structure. Often, power rates decline with consumption giving large discounts to high volume consumers. This type of structure provides an incentive to consume larger amounts of power because the marginal cost declines with rising consumption. Some communities in the United States have switched to a flat rate schedule, and the Government of India should consider this possibility for some consuming sectors.

Another change in the rate system which reduces the need for generating capacity is peak load pricing. There are a number of variants to peak load pricing. In one, higher rates are charged in times of system peak load to encourage consumption during off peak hours or seasons. In another variant, the rate for power depends in part on the peak load during each billing period. These pricing systems tend to reduce peak load and increase the effective utilization of existing capacity. The Government of India is studying the possibility of implementing peak load pricing systems in India.[1] This study should be given priority and a viable system of peak load pricing implemented as soon as possible.

Desirable as these policy options may be, they will not eliminate the power shortage in India. They should be pursued as a part of a coordinated package of policies to increase power availability in India.

ALTERNATIVE ENERGY SOURCES

Biogas

As explained in Chapter 6, biogas (methane gas) can be produced from cow manure and/or agricultural waste products. The residue retains the fertilizer qualities of the original materials so that potential fuel and fertilizer benefits can be derived from the inputs. Currently, the manure and agricultural wastes are used only for one of the two purposes. Commonly, cow dung is burned as a fuel and the fertilizer value is lost. This analysis concludes that there is significant potential for establishing biogas units in rural areas to increase fuel and fertilizer availability. The availability of biogas for cooking, some lighting, small industry, and operating irrigation pumps could significantly improve productivity and the quality of life in rural India.

1. G.o.I., *Fuel Policy Committee*, pp. 103-4.

A major problem with biogas production is that the technology is not sufficiently developed to achieve the full potential benefits. Further problems exist in designing units that are sufficiently reliable to be installed in villages throughout India. Required maintenance must be kept to a minimum, and repairs should be relatively simple. To achieve solutions to these technical and application problems, a rather large investment will be required. As one Government of India official stated, 'A quantum jump in biogas investment is needed to get the program off the ground'.[2] If this investment is made and the technical problems solved, biogas could become an important part of India's energy future.

Instead of consuming the biogas directly as fuel, the biogas could be converted to electricity and the energy consumed in this form. This process of decentralized power generation has been proposed as an alternative to centralized power generation. In Chapter 6, costs of the two approaches were compared and it was found that centralized power generation is more economical, at least for villages an average distance from main power lines. For more remote villages, power generation (and rural electrification) using biogas fuel may be a viable alternative. However, technical problems will have to be solved, and even then the rural electrification option may be less attractive than using biogas directly as fuel.

Whether biogas is consumed directly as fuel or converted into electricity, introduction of biogasification is likely to introduce social and institutional problems. The main beneficiaries of the new technology are likely to be the wealthier people in the village, while the poorest may even stand to lose in the process. The social consequences of introducing this new technology must be evaluated, and policy measures designed to prevent a worsening of the distribution of income.

Solar energy

Solar energy is an attractive future energy source because India receives a large amount of solar radiation. Research and development work has been initiated on using solar energy for home heating and for operating tube-well pumps for irrigation. At this point, these efforts do not have widespread application, but some prototype installations have been established. Solar energy has significant potential for India, although not for the next five years.

2. Interview with Dr. R. D. Deshpande, Department of Science and Technology, New Delhi, India, December 1975.

NON-COMMERCIAL ENERGY

About one half of the energy consumed in India is non-commercial energy which consists of firewood, dung, and agricultural waste products. By contrast, non-commercial energy consumption in the United States is negligible. The share of non-commercial energy consumption has been steadily falling in India since statistics were first compiled. This trend is expected to continue as development proceeds. Increasing rural electrification and the commercialization of village India will hasten this process. With progress in development, commercial energy will become more important and non-commercial energy less important.

Currently, the major policy issue concerning non-commercial energy is the rapid pace of destruction of India's forest resources for firewood consumption. The current rate of consumption is several times the maximum sustainable yield from India's forests. Recently, the rate of consumption of firewood has increased because of shortages and high prices of kerosene, a major substitute. If this rate of consumption continues, India faces potentially grave environmental consequences. Certainly, erosion will increase substantially and possible adverse climatic effects are even a possibility.[3] Some combination of the following policy measures should be considered to reverse the current trend:

1. Increase efforts to reduce the current rate of firewood consumption. Heavy penalties for public forest encroachment should be considered.
2. Initiate massive replanting programs with adaptable fast growing high yield species.
3. Devise incentives to encourage consumption of alternative fuels. One such incentive would be a heavy tax on industrial firewood consumption. Another would be removing the tax and increasing the supply of close substitutes like kerosene. With technical success in biogas generation, government subsidies for biogas production units is another possible policy measure.[4]

Another policy issue regarding non-commercial energy is how to make non-commercial energy transformation more efficient. As mentioned above, biogasification is one potential means of accomplishing this goal. Biogas can be burned much more efficiently than the original dung, and the residue is

3. Henderson, pp. 166-67.
4. Although these policy recommendations are the author's, they are based in part on information contained in G.o.I., *Fuel Policy Committee*, pp. 31-33; and Henderson, pp. 165-67.

valuable as fertilizer. Of course, energy is lost in converting the dung to biogas, and the technology for this conversion must be improved.

ENERGY AND THE ENVIRONMENT

Energy policy and environmental quality are very closely linked. Gordon MacDonald has stated this point as follows:

> The development of an energy policy is a key element in maintaining and improving the environment, because the use of energy effects the environment in an almost infinite number of ways. The conversion of fossil fuels to electricity produces thermal and chemical pollutants. The location of power plants raises the most complex of land use issues, and the production of raw fuels emphasizes similar questions of the use of land and natural resources. Beyond these serious but obvious questions lie the tremendously complex sociological and economic problems associated with the ever-increasing energy demands of our society.[5]

Accelerated development of energy supplies will definitely affect environmental quality in India. Offshore oil development leads to the possibility of oil spills. Coal development causes acid drainage from mines into streams. Air pollution results from the burning of coal. Hydropower causes little or no pollution, but it degrades scenic areas where plants are installed and where long transmission lines are erected.[6] Continued rapid depletion of forest areas will cause soil erosion, loss of soil nutrients, and possibly climatic changes. Consumption of cow dung directly as fuel has adverse environmental effects in that it pollutes the living area, causes eye discomfort or disease, and leaves a residue on clothing and other household surfaces.

In the first four five year plans, environmental quality was not mentioned in government planning documents. Neither was environmental quality covered in the *Report of the Fuel Policy Committee*. Environmental quality is listed as a subheading in the Fifth Plan, but the reference is to environmental improvements in city slum areas.[7] It is not that environmental quality is considered unimportant in India. Rather, it is that other development goals assume a greater importance. Environmental quality will become more important in India, as it has in other countries, when a higher level of development is achieved.

5. Gordon J. MacDonald, 'Energy and the Environment,' in *Energy, Economic Growth, and the Environment*, ed. Sam H. Schurr (Baltimore: Johns Hopkins University Press- for RFF., 1972), p. 100.
6. Edward S. Mason, 'Reconciling Energy Policy Goals,' in Schurr, p. 119.
7. G.o.I., *Fifth Plan*, 1: 90.

However, it is the view of this author that environmental quality impacts of major decisions should be considered even at this stage of Indian development. Undoubtedly, efficiency and equity impacts will still be weighted more heavily in most instances, but information on environmental quality impacts should become a regular part of the decision making process. Perhaps India can avoid some of the environmental problems now being experienced by more developed nations.

ENERGY POLICY RECOMMENDATIONS

One theme which runs through this analysis is that energy supply needs to be increased in India. The present high oil prices are placing a severe strain on India's balance of payments. Oil imports, even at the current reduced level, consume about 40 percent of India's foreign exchange earnings. Increased domestic oil supplies would help to alleviate this balance of payments problem and free foreign exchange resources for other vital imports.

Electric power shortages have been and continue to be a major constraint on growth in both the agricultural and industrial sectors. Substantial increases in power generating capacity are needed as quickly as possible to remove this constraint and stimulate future investment and growth.

To achieve increased power generation, coal production will have to be increased. If increased energy availability stimulates higher economic growth, coal demand as a direct input to the industrial and transport sectors will also rise.

All of these increases in energy production require large investments. Oil exploration and development, hydropower generation, and nuclear power generation are all highly capital intensive. Coal based thermal generation is also capital intensive, but not so much as the other sources. In addition, much of the investment in each of these sources must be in foreign exchange which is already scarce because of high world oil prices. To achieve all these production increases simultaneously would require massive increases in investment and foreign exchange allocation to the energy sector. It is unlikely that India could afford such shifts in investment given other development priorities. Even though it is not reasonable to shift sufficient investment to the energy sector to accomplish all of these objectives, some change in sectoral priorities is warranted. Given the close relationship of energy supply to economic growth, the sectoral allocation of investment funds should be reexamined, and the energy sector allocation should be increased.

The question then becomes one of setting priorities within the energy sector. The recommendation which evolves from this study is that heavy emphasis should be placed on the power sector. Unavailability of power has clearly constrained economic growth, and a massive investment in the power sector is needed to correct the current situation. Although hydropower investments should receive higher long term priority, for the short term, large investments in coal based thermal power should be undertaken. This course also requires increased investment for coal production in the near future.

It will be very tempting in India to avoid following this course and to concentrate on increasing oil production. The recommendation from this research is that India pursue a strategy of increasing domestic oil production by leasing offshore sedimentary areas to foreign oil companies. No doubt India could in time do this job herself and save all the oil production for India. The analysis of India's leasing system demonstrates, however, that India will be able to capture a large share of the oil (about 70 percent) by pursuing the foreign leasing path and not use any scarce foreign exchange or domestic investment resources in the process. These resources would then be freed for investment in other energy resources or other sectors of the economy.

For example, the budget increment for power generation discussed in Chapter 5 (Rs. 1618 crores) plus the additional investment required for coal production amounts to less than one fourth of the Fifth Plan *increase* in expenditures for oil exploration and development. India would be far better off to allow foreign companies to develop quickly her petroleum resources and lose a portion of the oil than to pursue a path of total self-development and spread the oil recovery over a much longer period of time.

An hypothetical example will serve to illustrate this argument. Assume that there are only four 500 million barrel oil fields yet to be discovered in India's offshore areas. Furthermore, assume that with a go-it-alone policy India could discover one of these fields every five years beginning in 1980. With a policy of leasing to foreign companies, we assume that two of the fields would be discovered in 1980 and two in 1985. Using the results of the leasing analysis, we assume that India would get (at no cost) 70 percent of the oil from the leased areas. Identical production streams for all fields are assumed, so for purposes of exposition we may utilize the discovered oil amounts. These assumptions are actually somewhat biased in favor of the go-it-alone policy. India would be unlikely to allocate sufficient resources to achieve such a relatively high rate of exploration and development for the go-it-alone case. Also, given the incentives for rapid exploration in the Indian leasing contracts, the foreign leasing policy would probably achieve a more rapid discovery rate than indicated.

Table 39 shows the discoveries (production) in absolute terms and present barrel equivalents (PBE) using a 10 percent discount rate. Even with this set of assumptions, the present barrel equivalent of oil produced using the foreign leasing strategy is slightly greater than that following the go-it-alone policy. This result is only in terms of physical volume of oil. The cost of oil in the foreign leasing policy option is borne entirely by the foreign companies (out of their share of the oil). The cost of the oil in the go-it-alone policy must be borne entirely by the Indian government. Hence, the advantage of the foreign leasing option is much greater than indicated in Table 39.

What this means for the energy sector as a whole is that India could concentrate on oil and natural gas development using the foreign leasing option and at the same time emphasize power development. In fact, only this type of combined strategy will loosen the energy bind on India. Resources are inadequate to follow a conventional balanced growth approach allocating some resources to each sector and sub-sector. This approach would continue shortfalls in all energy sectors. India can and should break the energy shortage cycle with massive investments in power and coal production. Development of the oil sector should be accomplished by leasing offshore areas to private firms using one of the capital recovery systems.

Table 39. Alternative policies for developing India's offshore oil resources.

	Go-it-alone policy		Foreign leasing policy		
Year	*Discovery*	*PBE*	*Discovery*	*Recovery*	*PBE Recovery*
	(Million barrels)			(Million barrels)	
1980	500	500	1000	700	700
1985	500	304	1000	700	425
1990	500	185			
1995	500	112			
Total	2000	1101	2000	1400	1125

In conclusion, India has good potential for providing adequate energy supplies for the future. If oil can be discovered and developed using foreign capital, adequate domestic resources will be available for investment in power generation as well as research and development on biogas and solar energy alternatives.

Selected bibliography

Ames, Glen C. W., *Some Causes and Consequences of the Petroleum Crisis on Agricultural Development.* Faculty Series, College of Agriculture, Athens: University of Georgia, 1974.

Arthur D. Little, Inc., *An Overview of Alternative Energy Sources for* LDCS. Report to U.S. Agency for International Development, Technical Assistance Bureau, Office of Science and Technology. Washington, D.C., August 7, 1974.

Auldridge, Larry, 'India Steps Up Exploration, Development.' *Oil and Gas Journal* (August 23, 1976): 50-53.

Bhargava, Mr. R. C., Department of Power, Ministry of Energy, New Delhi, India. Interview, December 1975.

Central Electricity Authority, *Ninth Annual Electric Power Survey of India.* Delhi: Government of India Press, 1975.

Chakravarty, Prof. S., Planning Commission and Chairman, Fuel Policy Committee, New Delhi, India. Interview, December 1975.

Chandra, Dr. Avinash, Monitoring and Evaluation Officer (Exploration), Ministry of Petroleum and Chemicals, New Delhi, India. Interview, December 1975.

Chaudhuri, M. R., *An Economic Geography of India.* New Delhi: Oxford and IBH Publishing Co., 1971.

Chaudhuri, M. R., *Power Resources of India.* Calcutta: Oxford and IBH Publishing Co., 1970.

Cheema, Mr. H. S., General Manager, Bombay High Operation, Oil and Natural Gas Commission, Bombay, India. Interview, December 1975.

Chitale, V. P. and Roy, Mrs. M., *Energy Crisis in India.* New Delhi: Economic and Scientific Research Foundation, October 1975.

Clawson, Marion, ed., *Natural Resources and International Development.* Baltimore: Johns Hopkins Press (RFF), 1964.

Dagli, Vadilal, *Natural Resources in the Indian Economy.* Bombay: Vora and Co., 1971.

Darmstadter, Joel; with Teltelbaum, Perry D.; and Polach, Jaroslav G., *Energy in the World Economy: A Statistical Review of Trends in Output, Trade and Consumption Since 1925.* Baltimore: Johns Hopkins Press (RFF), 1971.

Dasgupta, Biplab, *The Oil Industry in India.* London: Frank Cass and Co., Ltd., 1971.

Deshpande, Dr. R. D., Department of Science and Technology, New Delhi, India. Interview, December 1975.

Dutt, Mr. S. K., Science and Technology Specialist, American Embassy, New Delhi, India. Interview, December 1975.

Edison Electric Institute, *Statistical Yearbook of the Electrical Utility Industry for 1974.* New York: Edison Electric Institute, 1975.

Federal Energy Administration, *Project Independence Blueprint Final Task Force Report-Solar Energy.* Washington, D.C.: U.S. Government Printing Office, 1974.

Felix, Fremont, 'Growth of Energy Consumption and National Income Throughout the World,' IEEE *Spectrum* (July 1964): 81-102.

Fisher, Joseph L. and Potter, Neal, *World Prospects for Natural Resources.* Baltimore: Johns Hopkins Press (RFF), 1964.

French, Walter H., and Sanders, Gerald D., eds., *The Reader's Macaulay*. New York: American Book Company, 1936.

Geological Survey of India, *G.S.I. News*. Vol. 3, No. 4. Calcutta: G.S.I. Press, April 1972.

Geological Survey of India, *G.S.I. News*. Vol. 4, No. 7. Calcutta: G.S.I. Press, July 1973.

Geological Survey of India Officers, *Coal Resources of India*. Vol. 88. Calcutta: Pooran Press, 1971.

Ghosh, Alak, *Indian Economy: It's Nature and Problems*. 14th ed. Calcutta: World Press Private Ltd., 1970.

Government of India, *Economic Survey 1973-74*. New Delhi: Government of India Press, 1974.

Government of India, *The Fifth Five Year Plan in Outline*. Trivandrum: SGP at the Government Press, 1974.

Government of India, *First Five Year Plan*. Delhi: Government of India Publications Branch, 1953.

Government of India, *Report of the Energy Survey of India Committee*. New Delhi: Government of India Press, 1965.

Government of India, *Report of the Fuel Policy Committee*. Delhi: Government of India Press, 1975.

Government of India, Planning Commission, *Approach to the Fifth Plan 1974-79*. New Delhi: Government of India Press, January 1973.

Government of India, Planning Commission, *Draft Fifth Five Year Plan 1974-79*. 2 vols. New Delhi: Government of India Press, Vol. I 1973, Vol. II-1974.

Government of India, Planning Commission, *Fourth Five Year Plan 1969-74*. Delhi: Government of India Publications Branch, 1970.

Government of India, Planning Commission, *Notes on Perspective of Development, India: 1960-61 to 1975-76*. Delhi: Perspective Planning Division, 1964.

Government of India, Planning Commission, *Second Five Year Plan*. Delhi: Government of India, 1956.

Government of India, Planning Commission, *Second Five Year Plan: A Draft Outline*. Delhi: Government of India, 1956.

Government of India, Planning Commission, *Third Five Year Plan Summary*. Delhi: Government of India Publications Division, 1962.

Henderson, P. D., *India: The Energy Sector*. Washington, D.C.: World Bank, 1975.

Herfindahl, Orris C., *Natural Resource Information for Economic Development*. Baltimore: Johns Hopkins Press (RFF), 1969.

Herfindahl, Orris C. and Kneese, Allen V., *Economic Theory of Natural Resources*. Columbus: Charles E. Merrill Co., 1974.

Hirschman, Albert O., *The Strategy of Economic Development*. New Haven: Yale University Press, 1958.

Kalter, Robert J.; Tyner, Wallace E.; and Hughes, Daniel W., *Alternative Energy Leasing Strategies and Schedules for the Outer Continental Shelf*. Agricultural Economics Research Series 75-33. Ithaca: Cornell University, December 1975.

King, W. R., *Probability for Management Decisions*. New York: John Wiley and Sons, Inc., 1968.

Kumar, Mr. L., Advisor, Planning Commission, New Delhi, India. Interview, December 1975.

Kumaramangalam, S. Mohan, *Coal Industry in India*. New Delhi: Oxford and IBH Publishing Co., 1973.

Lakshmanan, M. S., *Economic Development in India*. Delhi: Hindustan Publishing Corp., 1974.

Lal, H., *Indian Petroleum*. New Delhi: Delhi Press for Lifeline Publications, 1963.

Lal, Sham, ed., *The Times of India Directory and Yearbook Including Who's Who*. Bombay: The Times of India Press, 1976.

Mahanti, P. C., ed., *Coal and Mining Review*, Annual Number, 1974.

Makhijani, Arjun with Poole, Alan, *Energy and Agriculture in the Third World*. Cambridge: Ballinger Pub. Co. for the Ford Foundation, 1975.

Mellor, John W., *The New Economics of Growth*. Ithaca: Cornell University Press, 1976.

Mikesell, Raymond F., *Public Foreign Capital for Private Enterprise in Developing Countries*. Essays in International Finance No. 52. Princeton: Princeton University, April, 1966.

Ministry of Information and Broadcasting, The Research and Reference Division (Government of India), *India: A Reference Annual 1975*. New Delhi: Publications Division, 1975.

Naegamvala, J. P., 'Power Outlook in the Western Part of the Northern Region: A Case for Rapid Hydro-electric Development.' *Indian Journal of Power and River Valley Development* (January 1975): 1-14.

National Committee on Science and Technology (Government of India), *Science and Technology Plan 1974-79*. 2 vols. Delhi: INSDOC, August 1973.

National Council of Applied Economic Research, *Demand for Energy in India*. New Delhi: N. K. Gossain and Co., 1966.

Nayyar, Mr. Vineet, Ministry of Finance, New Delhi, India. Interview, December 1975.

Nelson, Michael, *The Development of Tropical Lands: Policy Issues in Latin America*. Baltimore: Johns Hopkins Press (RFF), 1973.

Organization for Economic Co-operation and Development, *The Exploration for and Exploitation of Crude Oil and Natural Gas in the OECD European Area Including the Continental Shelf*. Paris: OECD Publications, 1973.

Parikh, Kirit S., *Second India Studies: Energy*. Delhi: McMillan Co. of India, Ltd., 1976.

Parikh, Kirit S., Director, Indian Statistical Institute and Member, Fuel Policy Committee, New Delhi, India. Interview, December 1975.

Parikh, Kirit S. and Srinivason, T. N., *Food and Energy Choices for India*. New Delhi: Indian Statistical Institute, August 1975. (mimeographed)

Petroleum Information Service, *The Indian Petroleum Handbook 1973*. New Delhi: Statistics Division, Petroleum Information Service, 1974.

Petroperu, *Peruvian Petroleum: Present and Future 1975*. Edited by Petróleos del Perú, 1975.

Prasad, C. R.; Prasad, K. Krishna; and Reddy, A. K. N., 'Bio-Gas Plants: Prospects, Problems and Tasks.' *Economic and Political Weekly* Special Number (August 1974): 1347-1364.

Rahman, Dr. A., Council of Scientific and Industrial Research, New Delhi, India. Interview, December 1975.

Rao, Mr. K. L. N., Superintending Geologist, Oil and Natural Gas Commision, Bombay, India. Interview, December 1975.

Revelle, Roger, 'Energy Use in Rural India.' *Science* Vol. 192, No. 4243 (June 4, 1976): 969-975.

Sankar, Mr. T. L., Secretary, Fuel Policy Committee, New Delhi, India. Interview, December 1975.

Sarah, Jasmin, and Guru, Jagat, *Indian Plans: A General Survey and Critical Study of First, Second, Third, and Fourth Five Year Plans*. Delhi: Universal Book Co., 1966.

Sathianathan, M. A., *Bio-Gas Achievements and Challenges*. New Delhi: Association of Voluntary Agencies for Rural Development, 1975.

Sen, Mrs. Anjali, Public relations officer, Coal India Limited, Calcutta, India. Interview, December 1975.

Singh, G. S., *Economic and Commercial Geography*. Bombay: P. C. Manaktala and Sons Private, Ltd., 1967.

Schurr, Sam H., ed., *Energy, Economic Growth, and the Environment*. Baltimore: Johns Hopkins University Press (RFF), 1972.

Stanford Research Institute, *Patterns of Energy Consumption in the United States*. Report to U.S. Office of Science and Technology. Washington, D.C.: Government Printing Office, January 1972.

Stamp, Dudley L., *Our Developing World*. London: Faber and Faber, 1968.

Sur, A. K., *Natural Resources of India*. Bombay: Padma Publications Ltd., 1947.

Tanzer, Michael, *The Political Economy of International Oil and the Underdeveloped Countries*. Boston: Beacon Press, 1969.

Thacker, M. S., *Natural Resources and Their Planned Utilization*. Baroda: University of Baroda Press, 1963.

Thompson, Dennis L., ed., *Politics, Policy and Natural Resources.* New York: The Free Press, 1972.

Tiwari, R. D., *Our Economic Resources.* Bombay: New Book Co., 1944.

Uhler, R. S., and Bradley, P. G., 'A Stochastic Model for Determining the Economic Prospects of Petroleum Exploration Over Large Regions.' *Journal of the American Statistical Association* No. 65 (June 1970): 623-630.

United Nations, Department of Economic and Social Affairs, *Mineral Resources Development with Particular Reference to the Developing Countries.* (ST/ECA/123), 1970.

United Nations, Department of Economic and Social Affairs, *World Energy Supplies 1970-1973.* Statistical Papers, Series J, No. 18, 1975.

United Nations, Educational, Scientific and Cultural Organization, *Energy in the Service of Man,* Paper No. 1, By Sir A. C. Egerton, Chairman (UNESCO/NS/74), February 13, 1951.

U.S. Department of the Interior, *Energy Perspectives,* by Herman Enzer, Walter Dupree, and Stanley Miller. Washington, D.C.: Government Printing Office, February 1975.

U.S. Department of the Interior, *United States Energy Through the Year 2000,* by Walter G. Dupree, Jr. and James A. West. Washington, D.C.: Government Printing Office, December 1972.

U.S. Geological Survey, *Geological Estimates of Undiscovered Recoverable Oil and Gas Resources in the United States.* Geological Survey Circular 725, 1975.

Vansant, Carl, *Strategic Energy Supply and National Security.* New York: Praeger Publishers, 1971.

Venkataraman, K., *Power Development in India.* New Delhi: Wiley Eastern Private Ltd., 1972.

World Bank (International Bank for Reconstruction and Development), Working papers (xeroxed). Washington, D.C.: March 1976.

World Energy Conference, *Survey of Energy Resources.* New York: The U.S. National Committee of the World Energy Conference, 1974.

Zimmermann, Erich Walter, *World Resources and Industries.* 3rd ed. Edited by W. N. Peach and James A. Constantin. New York: Harper and Row, 1972.

GPSR Compliance

The European Union's (EU) General Product Safety Regulation (GPSR) is a set of rules that requires consumer products to be safe and our obligations to ensure this.

If you have any concerns about our products, you can contact us on ProductSafety@springernature.com

In case Publisher is established outside the EU, the EU authorized representative is:

Springer Nature Customer Service Center GmbH
Europaplatz 3
69115 Heidelberg, Germany

Batch number: 10837190

Printed by Printforce, the Netherlands